Just Another Day at The Office

The true working memoirs of a Paramedic who was formerly part of a Bomb Disposal team in Belfast.

by

Chris Murkin

Bloomington, IN Milton Keynes, UK

authorHOUSE

AuthorHouse™
1663 Liberty Drive, Suite 200
Bloomington, IN 47403
www.authorhouse.com
Phone: 1-800-839-8640

AuthorHouse™ UK Ltd.
500 Avebury Boulevard
Central Milton Keynes, MK9 2BE
www.authorhouse.co.uk
Phone: 08001974150

This book is a work of non-fiction. Unless otherwise noted, the author and the publisher make no explicit guarantees as to the accuracy of the information contained in this book and in some cases, names of people and places have been altered to protect their privacy.

First published by AuthorHouse 1/25/2007

ISBN: 978-1-4259-8096-2 (sc)

Printed in the United States of America
Bloomington, Indiana

This book is printed on acid-free paper.

Dedicated To:

All Paramedics and EMT's up and down the country.

Glossary

Asystole	Flat line on the ECG (no heart movement)
A+E	Accident and Emergency department
'A' post	Front drivers side post . Between the drivers door and windscreen
BP	Blood pressure
Bi-Lateral	Equal movement on each side
Cannulation	To gain I/V access
Comms	Communication
CCTV	Close circuit television
CTL	Clinical team leader (team supervisor)
CPR	Cardiopulmonary Resuscitation
CVA	Cerebral Vascular Accident (stroke)
CX Collar	A neck collar to protect the cervical(CX) spine
DI	Daily Inspection of the vehicle and equipment
De-Fib	Defibrillator. Machine used to monitor the heart (ECG) and/or deliver an electric shock (joules) in cardiac arrest
ECG	Electrocardiograph (to look at the electrical movement of the heart, That little squiggly line!)
EMT	Emergency Medical Technician
EOD	Explosive Ordinance Disposal
Femur	The bone in the thigh
HGV	Heavy Goods Vehicle
INLA	International Liberation Army
IRA	Irish Republican Army
I/V	Intra-venous access
Joules	A measurement of electric/energy
Laryngoscope	A curved shape tapered 'blade', with a light set in it. Inserted into the throat to move the tongue away and give a visual contact with the Airway
MCQ	Multi Choice Question paper
MG's	Milligrams
Mil's	Millilitre

NSR	Normal Sinus Rhythm on an ECG (normal movement of the heart)
Oximetry	A measurement of oxygen within the blood
O2	Oxygen
OP Airway	Oropharyngeal airway. A curved hollow piece of plastic inserted into the mouth to hold the tongue away from the airway
OP	Operation
PTS	Patient Transport Service
POW	Prisoner of war
Red Call	999 call
RMA	Regimental Medical Assistant
RRV	Rapid Response Vehicle
RTA/C	Road Traffic Accident/Collision
RUC	Royal Ulster Constabulary
RV Point	Rendezvous point
Sit-Rep	Situation Report
TA	Territorial Army
T/F	True/false questions
Tachycardia	Fast heart rate
Tango Call Sign	Training crew
Tibia (Tib)	Lower leg front bone (the shin)
TLC	Total loving care
Wig-wag	Alternate headlights flashing on high-beam? Query (to question)

Acknowledgements

To my wife Lisa, Dave Nunn, Anthony Shepard, John Hargreaves,
Kathy and John Myer
Without their help this book would still be a ring binder.

Chapter 1

It was a dull, November morning. I hadn't slept brilliantly but then it was my first night as part of the British forces bomb disposal team in Belfast, "Felix" for short. The name apparently came from Felix the cat, nine lives and all that caper! The training had been a good 'crack', intensive but fun. Now it was time to be serious. It had been drilled into us in good' ole squaddie fashion that we were the enemy and were one of the highest targets for activist from the IRA and the INLA to name a couple. They weren't too happy that they had gone through all the trouble of building and deploying a bomb, just for us to come along and wreck it for them, umm, I could understand that.

At about 06:30am after a restless night I woke with someone shouting at me "Chris! Chris! GET OUT OF BED" In a startled panic I dived out of bed and gripped very hard in the area of the noise. I maintained my grip whilst banging the body up against the closest wall.

"Chris! What the bloody hell are you doing" Coming to my senses I realised it was Ginge, one of the bomb disposal team, oops. I guess the 'squaddie' talk had worked and I was about to trust no one.

"Get yourself sorted out we've got a Felix request"

"Shit, sorry mate" as I came to my senses. Thankfully Ginge knew me as we'd both been in the Regimental boxing team together. He was a good lad, good at what he did and had been recently promoted. He also knew I could be a bit feisty from time to time!

In the briefing room we got our location and were told there was a report of a suspected terrorist car bomb. Off we went a group of 20 year-old's, blues and two's wailing, no form of advanced driving and through the streets of Belfast that we didn't know. It was 7 o' clock in the morning, dark, wet, driving at break-neck speed in 1 ton armoured cars that were full of explosives, in an area where the 'locals' would like to shoot you. Surreal, just about describes it!

We arrived at a piece of Belfast scrubland. It had quite wide grass verges that had been worn down by something or other, with brown patches throughout. The rain was falling lightly and there was a smell of a coal fire burning somewhere. We pitched up in our 4 armoured cars about 100 metres away from the suspected car bomb still half asleep. In the gloom I could see a silver car standing on it's own parked on one of the verges and a factory about 200 metres behind it. Maybe that was the target? But it was along way away and it would have to be a powerful bomb to destroy or cause damage to it.

The quick exit from my bed had been done before, whilst on various exercises, but this time it was for real. This was no exercise and the phrase "you need eyes in your arse" was all too real. Looking around there were Squaddies all over the place. Some had been deployed as cover for us and some were those who had been deployed as an initial reaction force to the reported car bomb. I couldn't quite understand why someone would want to put a car bomb at this location. There was nothing worth blowing up, it was scrubland for god's sake. But who was I to question what was going on, it was my first job after being in Northern Ireland for all of 24 hours. We were all beavering away getting on with our various jobs. Mine was to make sure all the explosives were at the ready. We sent down one of the wheelbarrows (small, remote controlled, tracked vehicle). They have a couple of cameras fitted so you can have a good look at what you're dealing with. The pictures were sent back via the CCTV we operated. We could make out a milk churn in the boot of a virtually brand new XR3. There was only one way to deal with that type of device and it was good fun. In the back of my vehicle we had an explosive device which was about 2ft X 1ft and about 8"deep. It was packed with explosives which had got ball bearings glued into the top of it. Needless to say it packed a pretty heavy punch. We brought the 1st wheelbarrow back and sent the 2nd one down all rigged up with the explosives. They were placed under the boot of the car and the wheelbarrow reversed back to a safe distance.

"*Controlled explosion 1min*" Came over the radio. I looked at my watch and crouched behind the wing of the armoured car, camera in hand.

"*5, 4, 3, 2, 1, Fire*" KABOOM. The whole area seemed to shake whilst the XR3s back end came off the ground about 6ft with a huge fireball underneath it. The spare wheel exited through the rear window and went about 30ft into the air. All around us was this noise, chink, chink, chink, the milk churn had been blown to bits and fragments landed all around us. I waited for all the chinking to stop and gave myself a quick head to toe survey. Head, neck, shoulders, arms stomach, the packet! Legs and feet, all in tact, excellent. Looking back to where the car had been it was a total wreck, even the bonnet had opened itself. No windows left, even the metal sunroof had disappeared somewhere. There was a whole heap of wires hanging out in the driver's compartment. Wrecked, totally wrecked. Little did I know at this time that wrecked cars were going to become a big part of my future working career. I still couldn't understand why the car bomb had been placed here.

Once we got back to the barracks, we had a de-brief and I asked the question "What would have been the importance of blowing up that particular piece of waist land?"

Well apparently it was a stolen car from the previous night. This is quite common in the provence. What the thieves do after they've had a joy ride, is put a milk churn in the back of the car for all to see, it gets reported at some point as a suspected car bomb, we all go along and blow it to bits. Any evidence which may be in the vehicle gets destroyed, clever? No. The fact is the local RUC (Royal Ulster Constabulary) couldn't give a monkeys about a stolen car. This was Northern Ireland and they've got a few other problems to think about! However it was good training for us and the first time I had been put under any real pressure to perform in an emergency situation.

About an hour or so after we had been de-briefed, we sat in the main room all talking and laughing still quite high from the early morning activities. I took a look around the room. I was surrounded by people who I had some serious respect for. That morning we had all worked together and pulled off one of the biggest operations I had been involved in. I felt it had been the first time I'd felt part of a team, a real team that is. I had always been part of the regimental boxing, football and cricket teams, but somehow this was different. We couldn't afford to make any mistakes and we hadn't. We had to trust one another's judgement and we did. We had all walked away unscathed from a job that had gone like clockwork. The thought of someone putting their lives in my hands, quite frankly was a bit spooky!! But I enjoyed being put under the cosh in a situation where everything had to be done right.

A couple of months into the tour and we were the immediate team, which basically means we were the first team to deal with any calls that might come in. This happened every other day. The other team were on stand-by and so it alternated every 24 hours. It also meant 24 hours in 'combats' and me being a short arse, it meant being quite uncomfortable. One size fits everyone type attitude. It was about 1800hrs, dark and wet again. The phones rang and we all legged it to the ops room to find out what the call was, where we were going and what type of incident we were going to be dealing with. It was a street light in the middle of a bridge which was out and the wires were hanging out of the light cover, which was now ill fitting. That same old question kept springing to mind, why would someone want to blow up a street light? I couldn't get my head around it. OK so you might want to blow up a bridge for some form of tactical advantage but this bridge was in the middle of a hard catholic area. I suppose the bomb could have been put there by protestant freedom fighters to cause a bit of death and carnage but surely the locals would have identified them. However it was now our job to stop anyone getting hurt.

We pulled up at the location about 100 metres short of the bridge. We formed our usual diamond shape so we could work in the middle of the four vehicles. First of all for protection purposes and secondly to be out of the way of onlookers. Some of the kit we carried was classified and not for the public gaze. We sent the first wheelbarrow down and started to get the pictures back via the CCTV system. There wasn't a great deal to be seen as the front of the lamppost had been put back on. Our boss who was a captain decided he'd have to go down to the lamppost to take a closer look. As I started to get his bomb suit out, Ritchie, one of the guards we carried with us tapped me on the shoulder,

"Look over there"

As I looked I could see three people. One of them had a video camera against his eye "bloody onlookers" I spat back and continued with what I was doing.

"No you Pratt look again" I studied the figures a bit more closely this time.

"Bloody hell"

It was three high-ranking anti-Brit activists that we had been briefed about before

leaving for Northern Ireland. A shiver went down my spine. The boss came over to get his kit on as Ritchie and me were still digesting this information.

"Hold on Boss" I said "Take a look over there" Pointing in the direction of the video camera. He looked and then looked back at me.

"Well they ain't going to detonate the package whilst that lot are there are they, what ya reckon?" I thought for a minute

"I reckon you're right but also bonkers. What about the video?"

"Maybe they are expecting me to do an Irish jig for them at the same time" He replied in his usual arrogant way. As he pulled on the bomb suit I looked at Ritchie who put a finger to his right temple and rotated it as if to say, he's mad. This wasn't far from the truth! The boss went and done the usual thing which by now was becoming routine. He also did an x-ray which we could develop on scene. Nothing seemed to be too much out of order, so we cleared the area and handed back over to the RUC. During the de-brief back at the barracks we called a lad from the intelligence cell. We figured that the presence of the video camera was quite significant. However he was quite 'matter of fact' about the whole thing and wasn't really interested in what we were saying.

The following day we were on stand-by and after 12 o'clock we could put on sports kit and go to the gym, play footy or just generally doss. Personally I liked to get out for a run but we weren't allowed out of the barracks and it was only half-a-mile around the inner barrack perimeter. So that became very boring very quickly but it was better than being in combats. That evening shortly after our evening meal the phones rang. I wandered up to the ops room out of curiosity and boredom really, to find out where they were going. This also meant the combats had to go back on as we would now be the immediate team.

The call came through on the radio,

"*Zero to lima one one Bravo over*"

"*Lima one one bravo go ahead over*"

"*Zero, we have a Felix request to grid 310420 over*"

I thought I knew that grid reference. When I looked at the map my heart accelerated three fold. It was the same grid reference as we had been to the night before. Same bridge same lamppost.

"Oh shit" I muttered under my breath.

"What's up Chris?" Asked my equal from the other team.

"This grid you've got, it's the same place we went to last night when they were videoing us"

"Videoing?"

"Yeah, didn't the intelligence boys brief you this morning?"

"No" I tutted and I gave them a quick brief of what we had done, who was there, how we worked and most importantly our route and where we parked our vehicles in the diamond formation. I sat by the now unmanned bomb disposal radios. Comms are so important when there's an OP going on and if nothing else I would gain as much information as possible about the job. This was the first time I'd become worried/concerned about the tour. Up till now everything had gone without a hitch but I now questioned weather that was down to us being good at what we done or was it because the various anti-Brit factions had left us alone? Maybe it was our turn on the hit list. I listened to every communication that went between the bomb disposal team and zero (the person in charge). Just waiting for the shit to hit the fan, but all went smoothly. They returned to the op's room about two hours later. I sat down and listened to their de-brief. As it turned out they went to the opposite end of the bridge to us. They had picked up a bit of trouble en-route but nothing that you wouldn't expect when travelling through a hard catholic area. They had spent a lot of time scanning through various radio frequencies which could set off a radio-controlled device. But nothing was found. There also hadn't been any one there with a video camera but the guards had noticed the same three activists watching them. Was I over reacting? Something was occurring and the intelligence cell didn't seem to be too interested.

The next day we were once again the immediate team. We all felt a bit twitchy after what had happened over the past 48 hours and as a result it was the topic of conversation. There was a whole lot of speculation going on which wasn't helping any of us.

The following morning we had been out to a suspect package which we dealt with in our normal manner. After the controlled explosion we all got covered in dog biscuit crumbs! The package had been dropped accidentally and one of the locals had reported it as suspicious. It's a real piss off when you go tanking out to a job only to find it's nothing. If someone had used a bit of savvy the dog would have got its biscuits and we wouldn't have been called.

The day went by slowly. Springy, Ginge, Ritchie and me were making our way back from the cookhouse after tea when we heard the phones going off. We all legged it back to the digs, grabbed our kit and went into the ops room. It was now about 6pm and darkness was falling and you've guessed it, it was raining. In the ops room we listened to the radio as the call came through

"*Ground patrol x-ray Yankee to zero, you receiving over*"

"*Zero to x-ray Yankee go ahead over*"

"*Felix request to grid 310420 over*"

"*Zero to lima one one alpha you receiving over*" (Lima one one alpha was our call sign)

"*Lima one one alpha, Roger, Felix request to grid 310420, over*"

"*Zero, Roger to that, I'll leave you to it, over and out*"

I recognised the grid ref straight away, as did most of us. That bloody lamppost again.

I was beginning to wish we had blown it to bit's the first time we went near it. We had a quick pow-wow with the other team before getting our weapons and leaving the relative safety of the barracks. Our route was one that we wouldn't take on a normal journey. The idea being we would out-smart any plans which the activists may have of taking us out of the game en-route. At the end of the day there are only two ends to a bridge, both had been used up. Our options were limited and it was now a battle of wits between us and the activists, the unseen enemy. We had elected to diamond up in a cul-de-sac at the end of the bridge we had been to on the first call. We were able to pull down the cul-de-sac about 100 meters. This would leave us about 200 metres from the dodgy looking lamppost. As we pulled up we formed our diamond and got out of the vehicles. I expected to see the RUC controlling the usual crowd that would generally jeer and hurl abuse at us. On this occasion, nothing, an eerie silence almost The alarm bells weren't just ringing, they had now been joined by claxons as well. I wasn't sure where to look first. However I thought if it's going to happen then it's going to happen and there's jack shit I could do about it now.

Ritchie took up his usual position and we went about our work. The wheelbarrow was sent down and the same gloomy pictures were sent back. Nothing that could be done really. We armed the second wheelbarrow with a shotgun, sent it down and when only a few inches away from the lamppost we took a shot. Successfully the shotgun had taken the cover off of the lamppost. We sent down the first barrow with the cameras to take a look inside the lamppost. As the pictures came back there was no evidence of any form of explosives. The Boss umm'ed and arh'ed for a minute "I'm going to have to take a look, not that I particularly want to, but it's got to be done" I grabbed his kit out of my vehicle and assisted him to get it on. It was a two-man job as the suit was heavily padded and had a lot of bomb protection plates in it. Suddenly we heard a loud crack and whiz the boss stumbled forward losing his footing. I managed to hold him up and help him regain his balance.

"You all right sir"

"Just about, what the bloody hell was that?" We both turned. Ritchie was on the floor. No noise, no movement, nothing apart from a stream of blood seeping out of his head.

"Shit" I legged it over to where Ritchie was laying and arrived at about the same time as Ginge and Springy. I had done an RMA (regimental medical assistance) course during my time in Germany and as a result I was considered the medic of the team. But this was far greater than anything I'd dealt with before. Ginge got onto the radio

"*Lima one one alpha, contact!* (Army jargon to say you've been shot at) *One shot, one man down, wait out*"

"How is he Chris?" I looked at Ritchie with my torch. He was in deep shit. So white and he was loosing a mass of blood from the back of his head. I pulled off one of my gloves and checked for a pulse in his neck. I could feel a faint very rapid pulse and his chest was heaving, gasping for breath.

"He's in the shit Ginge, get us an ambulance mate"

"*Lima one one alpha, request an Ambulance at our location immediately over*"

"*Zero to lima one one alpha, roger to that, out*" I pulled Ritchie's helmet off and with my torch had a look at the back of his head. There was an area of skin missing about 6 inches square and what looked to be a hole in the back of his head. I got my water bottle and tipped it over the injury to try and clear the area and have a better look. There was definitely a hole about the size of my thumb. What else can I do I thought to myself. I pulled his field dressing from his webbing opened it up and made the best job I could of trying to stop him losing any more blood. I had no other form of med kit to call on. I put him in the recovery position, of course that helped! and kept checking his breathing which by now was very light and rapid. He was sweating like he was in a sauna with his pulse now virtually unreadable. The Ambulance crew arrived, cracked on and got Ritchie away from the scene. The rest of the job was all a bit dis-jointed but without incident, thankfully. By the time we got back to the ops room for our usual de-brief, there had still been no word on Ritchie but it was looking pretty grim on scene. On this occasion we were met by a senior member of staff this was always going to be bad news.

"Sit down troops" There was a slight pause while we got ourselves sorted out.

" I'm not going to beat around the bush, Ritchie is dead. That's life gentleman we are in a theatre of war and Ritchie is another casualty. You still have a job to do and a tour to finish. You all need to put this behind you and crack on. May the rest of your

tour be less troublesome. "Carry on sergeant" And left the bloody room. Well that was the de-brief finished with anyway!

We all went over to the choggies (On camp shop) that night and bought just a small amount of beer. We all sat around that night just talking no laughing, we got sooooo pissed. We never fell asleep we lost consciousness! 0600 came around all to soon. The following day I was in the radio room and wasn't feeling to good about myself I have to say. We found out that the bullet which had killed Ritchie had glanced off the back plate of the boss's suit, ricochet off of my vehicle and into the base of Ritchie's skull. They where obviously after the boss but had missed. Poor old Ritchie copped it instead. We were still shaken by the incident but if nothing else it was quick.

About 1330 the phone rang, "321 EOD" (explosive ordinance disposal)

Another Irish accent, this time cold, very cold

"I'm a representative from the - - - -"

"Good afternoon Sir"

"Last night you were called to a bridge with a light out"

"That's correct"

"In fact you have been there for the past three nights"

"Err, is that right?" The alarm bells had started again.

"Let's not play games young man"

"I'm listening"

"You unfortunately lost one of your comrades"

"Is that right"

"You know it's right"

"And your point sir?"

"And the point is this, you were lucky, so lucky. We've been watching you over the past week. Last night when you pulled in to your location, we had predicted that's where you would park and as a result we had deployed a command wire device, prepped for explosion in that area. Unfortunately for us it didn't explode. Now the device is still in situ and needs to be disarmed and removed before innocent civilians get injured by it."

"Let me make sure I've got this right."

I repeated the story back to him

"That's correct so it is"

"So last night you wanted to kill me, with a device that you now want me to go and dis-arm?"

"That's correct so it is"

"Are you a nutter? You killed one of my colleagues last night and now you want me to help you"

"Your comrade was another pawn lost to the game, that's unfortunate so it is but there's still a problem that needs to be rectified" I stood up and took a big drag on my cigarette. Another guy who sat in the radio room looked at me "You all right Chris"

"No I'm not"

"What's going on?"

" Bollocks mate that's what's going on, bollocks"

"Who, what, what's going on mate?" I picked the phone up again

"You there"

"Chris there's no need to be abusive" shit, he's heard my name! Another cold shudder went down my spine.

"Wait on the phone, I'll get my boss." I went into the boss and gave him the story. He asked me to put the call through to him. I was so angry. I had only joined the Army so I could get my HGV's. With my luck I should have known better! It took the rest of the tour for me to calm down. We had a meeting that night with the intelligence boys to try and form a plan together of how we're going to get this device away. We were all so pissed off with the whole episode that the intelligence boss wound up getting the flack for it! He said to leave it with him. As it turned out the SAS went in that night and cleared up the mess. Good lads.

The tour now behind me and I was due to leave the Army in a few months. The prospect didn't fill me with joy as there was 3.6 million unemployed. I had put myself about a bit with job applications, mainly for truck driving or van driving. My mum had said to me that the Ambulance Service was recruiting. So I stuck an application in to them as well but had no real desires to join. I was on my penultimate leave day about six weeks before I was due to leave the Army when a letter arrived for me at Mum and Dad's. It was from the Ambulance

Service saying I was a suitable applicant and could I go for an interview in 10 days Time. 'No' was my initial response but then I thought, I wonder if I could get some extra leave out of the Army? So I called my Staff Sergeant back in Germany and told him what was going on. "Under the circumstances that should be all right but leave it with me and I'll see what I can do. I'll give you a call back once I've cleared it" 'Excellent' I thought, I've got something out of them. Later that day I got a phone call from my sergeant major who I always got on with. He wanted to know where, when and who was running it etc. After giving him all the information he wanted he said "There's one condition" Here we go I thought, loads of guard duties coming my way when I get back.

"What's that then"?

"You make sure you get the bloody job"!

Chapter 2

I got myself all suited and booted up, Mum knocked up a bit of brekky and sent me on my way. The interviews were to be held at a local psychiatric hospital. I wasn't sure if that was planned for a good reason or not! Prior to all of us getting to the interview stage we had all been sent a pre-learning pack about something called entonox, a painkiller by all accounts. This pack I learnt inside out and back to front. I was quite intrigued by the whole thing, "laughing gas", Gucci!

There were about 40 of us to start with. The first thing we had to do was a multi-choice question paper. Sixty Questions broken into 3 sections, Maths, English and General knowledge. We were given an hour to do the paper, a complimentary brew and then we had to go in individually and meet "entonox"! The Cylinder had been dismantled and there were various bits all over the floor. The instructor introduced himself shook my hand "Do you recognize what's in front of you"? I was half tempted to say no. The one I saw in the pre-learning pack was in one bit, however I played the game "yes I think so" Could you put it together for me then? I spent a few seconds remembering what I had read and tried to relate it to this pile of metal and rubber on the floor. I went about my business, slowly but precise with what I was doing. Once it was all together I held it up and had a look around the equipment just to be sure I hadn't forgotten anything. Then I remembered whilst reading the pre-learning pack there had been reference to decompressing the cylinder before offering to the patient. I squeezed the decompression valve and the cylinder made this horrible screeching whooshing sound, a bit like someone putting a big breath into a balloon. "Oops, is it supposed to do that"? The instructor laughed "Yes that's fine"

He then pinged a load of questions at me about the kit, what it does, what it doesn't do

etc. I answered to the best of my ability but didn't feel particularly confident. But then

I thought bugger it, I'm only in this for a few days extra leave. We were all told to go and get some dinner whilst the instructors marked our exam papers. As we walked out of the building I noticed a hearse. So I turned to the guy next to me and laughingly said, "someone's brought the family car I see"

"That's mine"

"What"

"That's mine"

"You a funeral director or something then"?

"No, it's my family car"

He was serious, it was his family car. Because it had so much room in it he could get all four kids and his wife in it at the same time. Fair play to the bloke I thought.

After dinner we all went into a main room. We were told that time was running short and as a result rather than putting everyone through the interviews they would say who had failed and they would be asked to leave. I thought that was a bit off really. I'd been talking to most of the other job hopefuls that were there and some had waited a long time to get a shot at being in the service. Now it could all be over with a role call. My past experience with that type of call was usually reserved for those in the crap. I wasn't too fussed, the extra leave made everything worthwhile but there was a pang of sympathy for those about to get binned. There was no messing about "The names which are called out if you could go into the other room and the rest of you remain here" I figured that the names which were called out and had to go into the other room, were those who had got through thus far. Well you didn't need to be Einstein to work out that that room had no outside door. As the names got called out one by one it was the first time I noticed that everyone was being called Mr this, Miss that and Mrs the other. 'Blimey' I thought, adults, were being treated like adults. Eventually all the names had been called and all those applicable had retired to "the other room". My name wasn't one of them. I felt this huge aura of disappointment flow throughout my body. I had failed. I was gutted although I'd only been there, in my eyes just to get a few extra days leave out of the Army. I was seriously pissed off with myself for failing and the personal disappointment was eating away at me. The instructor looked up at all of us who were left "If you could all follow me please" and went into another adjoining room. We all followed dutifully. The mood was sombre as I think everyone felt the same way I did. The instructor went on to say "If you could all take a seat please" We all sat waiting for the final curtain to drop and go back to our various day jobs. It was still reasonably early afternoon and I thought, uum at least the pubs would still be open. I could hook up with Docky (a good mate of mine since junior school) and go and get smashed. But it didn't seem to ease the disappointment I was feeling.

The instructor started with his mini speech "Sorry to be the bearer of bad news but someone has to do it. Unfortunately you will all have to sit around for a while and wait to be called through for your interview. Congratulations" I was stunned, we had all got through to the interview phase. I felt this big ole cheesy grin come on and virtually split my face in half. Looking around the room everyone was doing the same. Nice one troops I thought, nice one.

The interview was as you'd expect, lasting about an hour. With the usual poignant questions, views on life, different races, cultures, types of people. Why you wanted to be in the Ambulance Service and that question everyone hates "why do you think we should offer you the job"? I haven't got a clue what my answers were but it seemed to go ok. The journey home was only about 15mins and I felt I'd been back in the boxing ring once again. It had been a long day so I contacted Docky and we went out and got smashed anyway. Who needs commiserations!

About two weeks later and back in Germany I phoned home. Mum, as enthusiastic as ever said there was a letter with the Cambridgeshire Ambulance Service crest on it and could she open it? As Mum read on it was a letter offering me a job with a start date in November. I was chuffed to bits. I couldn't believe I had been offered a job with the emergency services. However the truth of it was, that I was going to be doing non-emergency work only-PTS (patient transport service). But the aim was to get a job and with 3.6 million unemployed any form of security was more than welcome.

I left the Army in September 1985 on good grounds with the Squadron Sergeant Major. He even said that if the job didn't work out to phone him within six months and he would have me back in the unit. That was ultimate security! Leaving the barracks for the last time was a sad day but it had to be done. I had become disillusioned with what was going on and fed up with the constant bullshit which had increased with a new Officer Commanding in Post.

The village where I had been brought up had a haulage firm in it and I'd joined the Army with the aim to get my HGV's, this I'd achieved. After being in Civvi Street for a week I was getting bored. So I wondered down to the local haulage firm and asked if they had any jobs going. I knew a lot of them as I used to play down there when I was a kid. They asked what licenses I had and then asked if I could start tomorrow? No problem.

The following day I was up nice and very early! Along with my older brother, Gary, who also worked there. Good' ole Mum was also up very early preparing brekky for us both, bless her. So off I trotted to do the truck-driving thing which had been my aim with the Ambulance Service well out of my mind. A month had gone by and I was in High Wycombe, Friday evening, 5:30ish dropping off my last load of the day. A 56-gallon drum filled with resin type stuff. I went and spoke with the receptionist who was busy finishing things off and she informed me that the forklift driver had knocked off for the day. This presented a problem or two. Problem (1), if I didn't shift this drum I was going to be stuck until 9am the next morning and (2), I was due at a do at the local pub that night for a party. Answer, to get the drum off myself. The receptionist said she would be happy to sign for it if it was in their warehouse. I set about tipping the drum off the side of my flatbed trailer. I moved it as close as I could to the side of the trailer, got off, grabbed the top of the barrel and pulled it towards me. As I did so I tried to stop it falling directly to the ground by letting it down slowly. I didn't have the physical strength to stop it falling. At that time I didn't realise it weighed a quarter of a ton! I tried to escape form underneath it by jumping backwards but unfortunately gravity worked with the weight far quicker than I could. I managed to move my head out of the way but the barrel struck me in the chest pushed me over and landed on my right leg with a big ole crack. That hurt!. I managed to push the barrel off and stood up.

I knew that something wasn't quite right and from all the various sports that I played I had developed a way of getting over the pain quickly. This was by stamping the injured leg on the ground. Whilst this would initially cause extreme pain I found when I stopped stamping the pain didn't feel half as bad and was able to continue, diverse I know! This I did several times. I decided to stop when I found it was making me feel nauseas. I sat on the barrel and started to gather my thoughts but also started to feel dizzy. So I laid myself on the floor with my head on the barrel as a handy sort of pillow. I now figured that walking was out of the question and someone would be along shortly. Sure enough someone came walking up the footpath where I laid.

"sorry mate could you give me a hand up?" he stepped around me and went on his way, what a git!.

The way I'd parked my truck I'd left the back end hanging out and as a result a Transit Van couldn't get by and decided to hang on his hooter

"piss off you Pratt" I yelled in his general direction. About 20 seconds later a head popped around the cab of the truck "you all right mate?"

"No not really"

"what's happened?" We were then joined by the receptionist who had heard me hurling abuse at this chap "you all right my love? Is there anything I can do?"

"I wouldn't mind a brew if that's possible" Off she toddled to put the kettle on. In the mean time the driver of the Tranny helped me up and sat me back on the barrel.

Sure enough a brew arrived and I sparked a cigarette up, bliss.

"listen mate you really need to get that leg looked at"

"it'll be ok in a minute, it just needs a bit of time to settle down"

"can I take a look at it? I work up the local hospital as a porter"

"go on then" he went to lift up the trouser leg and couldn't due to the swelling

"take a look at this mate" I looked down and realised that my Army lightweight trousers were tight with the swelling that had formed. Umm this was a new one on me. All my sports injuries had never created swelling like this before.

"I think you need an ambulance mate"

"no"

"well at least let me take you up the hospital, I think you may have broken your leg "

"no I'm sure I'll be fine"

"you really ought to have it x-rayed" this I figured may not be a bad move. The pain was slowly increasing and eventually I succumbed and agreed to go and have an x-ray.

He sorted my truck out, got the all-important signature and I hobbled into the back of his tranny van.

The doctor put the x-ray up on the screen that was behind me and over my left shoulder. He remained seated in front of me and looked at the x-ray from quite a distance. I thought that's ok then just a sprain, get back to my truck, get home and get partying. "is it ok if I take a look? I've never seen an x-ray close up before"

"by all means feel free" I turned round and looked at the dark/light image before me that were the bones in my leg "bloody hell" I remarked

"yes, you don't need to be a doctor to spot that one do you" My leg had snapped in two. All that stamping around lark had just crashed the ends of the bone together and created that much pain I'd almost passed out. Shan't be doing that again! I was wheeled off to the plaster room and up to the ward. Never did get to the pub.

Mum and Dad came and got me the following day and took me home. Mum did her usual and knocked up a bit of brekky. She also got me to phone the Ambulance Service and let them know I wouldn't be joining as soon as expected. They were very good under the circumstances "let us know when you're out of plaster and we'll give you another start date" I still had no intention of joining the Ambulance Service but nothing wrong with keeping your options open.

It was quite a few weeks before I could get back to work and by now it was December. Cold dark mornings and frost-covered canvases had to be unfolded and put over the various loads I was carrying. Being the new boy I also had all the crap that no one else wanted including the vehicle I was driving. When they went and recovered the lorry from High Wycombe the mechanic who drove it back recommended it be scrapped. The firm duly did and gave me the sister ship to it, which was equally as bad. It was difficult to drive and uncomfortable to sleep in to the point where the roof leaked.

I had a rush job up to Newcastle which took me 3 days by the time I had driven up in the bucket of crap, collected other loads and got back to the depot. I finally got back at about 8 o' clock at night thoroughly pissed off with this entire driving lark. It was policy that if you got back after the office staff had knocked off, you automatically started at 7am the following morning. So I got myself down to the depot and found I had the joys of London to drive around all day. I got my vehicle loaded, which took about an hour and by that time the office staff had started to arrive. I made my way into the office which was basically a serving hatch us truckies had to look through to talk to the office staff "Morning, I've got some invoices here for you" and handed them over. The transport manager went ballistic at me for making my initial drop 30mins late. He called me all the names under the sun and went on and on and on shouting. I felt myself boiling up and getting angry but rather than arguing I walked out and got myself a brew and a smoke. As I sat their gathering my thoughts, I thought, cheeky sod, I don't need this job. So I went back to the office "OI LOFTY, if that's your attitude there's a truck there going to London, suggest you find a driver for it, cause I'm out of here" I went to my truck grabbed my bag and my dog and went home.

I got home about 8:30, mum said "that was a quick day" subtle as ever. So I told her what had happened whilst she knocked up 'more brekky!' Afterwards she said about phoning the Ambulance Service as they've still got a job for you. I felt a bit guilty about phoning them as I knew there were people who badly wanted to join the service and hadn't got in, basically I wasn't too bothered. But a job is a job at the end of the day, and I was now unemployed with Christmas only a matter of days away. So I phoned the service and got through to the personnel department

"hi there my name is Chris Murkin, I was due to start on the 19th November but unfortunately I broke my leg. I was told to phone back when I was fit again which I now am"

"Hold on a minute" the usual irritating music started which always happens when someone is talking about you.

"Chris are you able to start on January 14th?"

"No Problem" which meant all of Christmas off plus another week, none too shabby really! As for all you truckies out there- RESPECT.

Chapter 3

Following a brief induction course lasting a week, I was given my own Ambulance and was to work on my own. This amounted to collecting out-patients from the local area and taking them for physiotherapy appointments, occupational therapy and some sadder cases which had gone through nervous breakdowns, or off to the local drug rehabilitation unit. After a few months of this I got a crewmate, a guy called Phil.

Phil was also an ex-squaddie so we had a lot in common and had a seriously good laugh when at work. One of the first patients we picked up was a patient called Mr Tower. He'd had a stroke (CVA) and was now wheelchair bound and going for some physio in an attempt to get him back on his feet. His first words to us were

"I haven't met you lads before you must be new boys" En-route to the out-patient department I told him a bit about my history, ex-squaddy and all that. He went on to tell me about when he was in the Army during the war, as so many of our patients had been. He told me this incredible story about him and six others that had been POWs in Italy. They managed to escape, build a raft and managed to get across to Sicily. At that point we had arrived at the Out Patient Dept and had to drop him off. Later that day we picked him up again to take him home. He continued with this amazing story of how they evaded capture and how they worked out their route with out the aid of map or compass. He was still telling the story when we had arrived at his home. We got him into his living room and I said that I would get the final instalment when we pick him up tomorrow.

The following day we started our journeys as usual and finally got to Mr Towers home. We knocked at the door which his wife answered.

"Morning, we've come to pick up Mr Tower"

"I'm sorry my dear he's not going in today. I have phoned hospital"

"Oh sorry about that. Well give him our regards and tell him I still want to hear the final part of his story"

"Unfortunately he passed away in his sleep last night" I didn't know where to put myself, I wanted the ground to swallow me up. Bless her at that point she started to cry. I did what I could to console her but was a bit inexperienced to say the least.

After a few minutes a friend arrived and took her in for a brew, leaving us to get on our way. The mood in the cab was solemn. We felt a right pair of prats putting our foot in it like that and we never found out how far Mr Tower and his friends got.

I'd been on Patient Transport Services (PTS) for about nine months. It was all right but after coming from Bomb Disposal it was a bit quiet for me and as a result I was now looking for another job. One morning one of the other PTS staff came up to me and said "are you putting in for one of the front line jobs?"

"Front line? I can't put in for that I don't have a lot of medical qualifications"

"Of course you can, they'll teach you all you have to know on a course"

"You sure?"

"Yes, you don't need any medical qualifications"

"you sure your sure?"

"YES, you'll be taught what you need to know"

"well why not then" go for it I thought, nothing to lose.

There were six of us from within the station that had applied for three positions on front line vehicles. I knew the training officer who was in charge of allocating the positions was an ex-squaddy and had some ties with the local TA Squadron. A lesson all Squaddies are taught in basic training is that 'bullshit baffles brains'. So it was maximum bullshit time, boots bulled, interview suit pressed to razor sharp condition and the service issue twat-hat brushed with the peak also bulled to mirror condition. I sat to attention, as bizaar as it sounds. With my twat-hat tucked neatly under my arm. The questions came thick and fast. There was no medical questions but more along the lines of scenarios and situations, such as, if you'd been on a job with your crewmate and the job was done different to how you wanted it to go, what would you do about it? And how do you feel about working with local Emergency Doctors and Volunteer services such as St John's and Red Cross? How do you feel about working night shifts? I answered all to the best of my ability with various explanations. Once again the interview lasted about an hour and at the end of it I was back on the road to my usual afternoon runs, no chilling out time.

We had to wait about a week to get the result. Now I had got myself to a point where I really wanted to get onto the front line vehicles. Having no idea that I was able to apply for such a job it was what I really wanted to do. It was a long week we had to wait and finally news came through. It was going to be Phil, one other lad and myself. I was over the moon that not only had I got one of the positions but also I was going to be away with Phil. What a laugh that was going to be. Phil had been on leave the day we found out the news so I phoned him that night to say well done and let's look forward to a top course. Unfortunately things had changed that day. Little did I know but one of the other people that had gone for the interview had chucked her teddy in the corner and complained that she should be favoured over Phil. I don't know the ins and outs of what went on but there were lots of girly tears and the initial decision was changed. This meant going away for eight weeks with someone who I didn't really get on with and who had got my mate binned off the course, we didn't gel!

The course was held at Pelsal, West Midlands. The training school had been purpose-built. With on site facilities, dining hall, classrooms, various buildings around for all sorts of scenarios. There was a basement which was used on a lot of occasions to make life as difficult as possible for casualty removal. It housed all the boilers so was hot and dusty. Most people didn't like scenarios in the basement but I liked being put in difficult situations and having to work out the best possible lifting techniques along with casualty treatments. Pelsal also had a social room consisting of a Pool table, bar billiards, jukebox and to top it all a BAR! Unfortunately someone

had forgotten to re-new the license so the bar wasn't open for alcoholic beverages, DOOH! but Probably not a bad thing as we had such a lot of information to take in and a muzzy head was not the order of the day. We all had our own rooms with brew facilities and all had been finished off with a recent lick of paint. It was a far cry from the usual training facilities I had been used to in the past.

We covered all aspects of pre-hospital care; from diabetic illnesses to home births; from drug overdoses to RTA's (road traffic accidents). We went into all the various bodily systems, respiratory, cardiac, digestive, nervous, circulatory, and skeletal. We also covered moving and handling techniques, examination and assessment of conscious and unconscious patients, airway management and resuscitation techniques. The list seemed to be endless. The four final written exams all carried a pass mark of 80 or 85%. Cardio Pulmonary Resuscitation (CPR) had a pass mark of 100% and there was no wavering from it. All the CPR exams where done with a machine which would give a read out at the end of the exam. It also gave a mark out of 100. if you didn't get 100 you failed and there was no going back. As the instructors kept saying to us "you won't get a second chance when you're on the road"

We all spent a lot of time with resusi-anne and got to know her quite intimately. I had never taken a shirt off a female so many times with so many onlookers. The eight weeks seemed to pass in as many days and finally it was crunch time. We were all nervous with the exams and for some students failure meant no job. For me failure meant back onto PTS work again. The thought of going back to PTS had probably pushed me on as well as possible. Also passing meant a further three-week driving course that I was really looking forward to.

As the names were called out we had to file into another room one by one where we were given our results. I was reasonably confident with the practical skills but unsure about the theory side of the exams. I had never been a great academic. My name was called and off I went into the room where no one had returned! I remembered the test and interview stage when I had first applied for the Ambulance Service but this was a whole lot more serious. All those who had been given their results went outside along the edge of the building and in to another room. I knew that one person had failed as we could hear the shrieks of emotion that followed. The poor instructor had his work cut out with her. I was called forward. As I went into the room my heart was in my mouth and it felt like it was going 200 miles an hour. I was asked to sit down.

"there's no easy way to tell you this" the instructor said, "you've done well on your practical work but take a look at your theory results"

As I looked down at the results I couldn't believe what I was seeing, 80%, 81% and the other two exams where 85% and 87%. "phew that was close"

"very close. What we recommend you do, is when you get back to your station you continue reading, if nothing else just to firm up what you have learned. Good luck with your driving course"

I walked out of the room and into the fresh air. I sat on a little wall just outside of the room where we were to go into once we had our results. I tried to take in how close it had been and to calm down a bit before joining the others. I sparked a cigarette up and gazed into space. A guy called Geoff who I'd got on with extremely well came out to where I was sitting and brought me a brew. It had become a standing joke on the course that if there was a brew somewhere I wouldn't be to far away.

"you ok"

"yeah not too bad, cheers"

"did you get through all right?"

"I did" and told him my results

"that was close"

"yeah I know but at least I'm through"

" Look forward to the driving course eh?"

"Too right, we'll have to get into the same group, give those cars a right hammering"

"no"

"NO!" I looked up and his face said it all, "what the bloody hell happened"

"I bombed out on one of the short answer papers. I only got 75%"

"what and no chance of a re-sit?"

"no 3% that's all you're allowed if you're going to take a re-sit"

"what now Geoff ?"

"unemployment" Geoff was one of those that had no job should he fail.

"Bloody hell Geoff, what are you going to do now"? Geoff shrugged his shoulders

"Don't know really Chris. Guess I'll go back and deliver parcels"

"You're not going to let all this lot drop surely. You've come too far just to forget about it. Either way you think about it Geoff, you've gained a lot of knowledge and just to waste it is ludicrous. Can you not have a word with your governor and see if you can sit it all again?"

"Yeah I'd thought of that. I haven't got anything to lose so I'll give it a try but I don't hold out to much hope" with that he started to well up. I felt so guilty. There was me licking my wounds because I had just scraped through and someone like Geoff who had failed on a written paper bringing a brew out and asking me if I was all right. Bloody hell.

Note to self, think of all those around you and not just yourself.

The end of training do was a little bit subdued out of respect for those who had failed. The only saving grace was that the bar had got its license back. We all had the weekend off and then it was back for the driving course. This consisted of a watered down version of the police pursuit-driving course. There was more theory than I expected but it was good fun. I'd spent a few years banger racing so had a pretty good idea of how vehicles would handle when put into a skid. Out on the streets of West Midlands and Wales. The rules were, that we could break the speed limit but if anything happened it was our fault and we would always uphold 30mph and 40mph speed limits. Over and above that we could do what we wanted. It was still intensive and the three weeks soon past. It was immense fun particularly the skid car. This was basically a framework that we put under the car with castors on each corner. The instructor had the ability to raise one corner or two or three or all four if he wanted to, from inside the car. It was a really fun day with the emphasis on learning how to control a vehicle when it had gone out of control. At one point I was doing about 70mph down a runway with a slight right-hand bend in it. As we started to turn right the instructor lifted the car off the ground but just enough so that the wheels kept slight contact with the road. I locked the steering wheel fully over to the left to steer into the skid. Now at full lock the car was controlled but it was still very sideways. After about 100mtrs of this I turned to the instructor and said "ok there is nothing else I can do" he looked at me with a rye grin and answered "what about if you now come off the ice?" he promptly dropped the car to full traction and we spewed off to the left at 90o. I thought the car was going to tip over. I turned hard right and as the car straightened up I braked and brought it to a stop in a straight line. "Not bad" the instructor said

"But remember, always prepare yourself for the unexpected"

Our various instructors from the various regions we came from had joined us all. This added to the pressure of the final 24 hours. We had two days of driving tests at the end of the driving course. We had a day drive where the instructors wanted to see the vehicles driven "progressively", this led onto a night drive. My night drive was with an Irish instructor who I hadn't met before. But he was renowned to be a complete git. My history and the Irish had got off to a bad start to say the least. But this was now Civvy Street and the past was the past. We met each other at about 0030. He was short with grey hair a bit of a weasel looking guy who wouldn't be out of place on the streets of Belfast. With this broad Irish accent he said "good morning to you young man" The voice sent shivers down my spine.

And all those pictures of the dark rainy bridge in Belfast and Ritchie's head came flooding back.

"Morning"

"I believe you have something to prove to me tonight?"

"You could say that"

It was a dark night with no moon to light the way. There was a slight drizzle to add the odd bit of excitement to the drive and I was given a Ford Granada. A car I had never driven before. The roads were slippery and caution was the order of the night.

We set out on our drive through Birmingham and then onto the motorway. On to some little country roads and then back onto the motorway. When we got closer to home we started to drive on more of the country roads. I was towards the end of my driving assessment and I thought I was going great guns. It was quick, controlled and I was reading the road ahead. At this point the instructor looked out of the window and muttered "I can see the grass growing outside" I couldn't believe it. I was going as quickly as I could without putting him, the car or me at risk. Bugger it I thought, this is showdown time. As the next half-hour or so panned out I gave the car so much grief I thought I was going to fail. I never had the car's back end hanging out totally but with a rear wheel drive, the rain as it was, I was getting close. As we pulled into the training school I thought I've blown it because I let the little Irish git wind me up. I pulled into the parking space and waited for the bad news. There were a few questions about the Highway Code which by now was second nature. Finally he said "well done, that was a bloody good drive. Mind you, don't get carried away when your in a real hurry and be aware that rear wheel drives can catch you out in the wet."

What a git, he was trying to make me make a mistake. That entire lark about watching the grass grow was just to see how I would do under pressure, when the shit was hitting the fan and I needed to get to hospital ASAP. Well fair play to the guy he had put me under pressure, maybe not for the reasons he thought though.

The bar was still open although it was well into the small hours. It is policy apparently that when the final driving tests are on the bar stays opens until late. As I was the last to go out of our group I was the last to hit the bar along with this instructor. All the others which had been in my car had also passed. There was one failure from the other car but all things considered it was still going to be a boozy session. We had now gone through 11 weeks of seriously intensive training.

There was only one failure amongst us and he wasn't to bothered. His Dad owned a computer firm in Birmingham and that was where he was off to work. Realistically he was going to be earning a lot more money than we could and he seemed happy enough. The following morning we had our local instructors present for the formal pass/fail results, although we already knew what they were. There was a quick de-brief and then we were all let loose to our own counties as fully trained, trainees!

Although we had gone through 11 weeks of intensive training and passed, we now had a 12 month period as a trainee. Every three months we were to have an assessment with an instructor to make sure we had taken on board the knowledge we had been given and that we weren't a danger to the public. But either way we were now operational.

Chapter 4

Another semi-sleepless night was had. Monday morning was only hours away and I was going to be operational, the first day on the road proper. One of the girls who had been on the course with me and myself were going to be with an instructor for the next five days. It was bad enough being on the road for the first time but with an instructor present this seemed to add to the pressure. I arrived at the station early, I couldn't see the point of lying in bed thinking about it. The station consisted of the main garage about 50ft X 100ft, of steel construction all painted a lovely colour of grey. There was two rows of vehicles parked on either side. On one side was the PTS vehicles and on the other side was the A+E (Accident and Emergency) vehicles. It had two roller doors one at either end. One in and one out. Through a set of double swing doors that led into the main corridor that linked the crew room with the garage. Just on the right was the main radio, which would encode the station and call the next vehicle out. Continue through the crew room and you arrive at the most important room in the building, the kitchen. Ninety-nine percent of the staff are part of the social club which left us with a constant supply of tea, coffee and the usual condiments to complement the best fish N chips money could buy, which is the staple diet of most front line crews! At the other end of the building were all the managers. Station officer, assistant chief, the chief ambulance officer plus all their secretaries. As a result no one ventured up there very often! The station itself was built in the early 70s and donned the very 70s décor, with wood panelled doors and basic paintwork, most of which was good ole magnolia and had seen far better days. Also up the corridor were the usual toilet facilities (male and female) with showers for those mucky jobs. The only other room of interest was the day stores. Just inside the double swing doors on the left. This was a room about 10ft X 8ft and was open to everyone. It kept a constant supply of dressings, plasters, splints, etc that would be used and replaced on a regular basis.

I went through to the kitchen, put a brew on and settled myself down. I tried to look like I hadn't had a sleepless night and waited for my crewmate and the instructor to arrive. One of the old boys came up and said "how ya feeling"

"Crap"

"Yep, I can understand that. It's not like another day at the office eh"

"You could say that"

This conversation was a milestone in itself. Generally speaking the A+E crews had nothing to do with PTS crews and conversation was kept to a minimum if they happened at all. Maybe after 12 months and getting the A+E course under my belt I was to be accepted.

My crewmate and the instructor arrived and we got allocated our vehicle. We started our DI (daily inspection) of all the equipment on the vehicle. Traction splint, box splints, IV stands (also known as fire fighters! Sorry boys) resus-bag (first response bag to any incident) O2 + masks, paediatric, adult, nebulising, 24%, 28%, 100%. Ventilator, suction + catheters, dressings, blankets, lifting aids such as KED's RED's and orthopaedic stretcher (Scoop for short). This is an aluminium framework which splits in half long ways and enables us to build a stretcher around a patient with minimum movement. Ideal for spinal injuries and used as a lifting aid for heavy/awkward patients. It also comes with a set of straps which are put in place in a criss-cross fashion across the body to stop patients moving around when being lifted up out of holes and lorries on their side etc. It's also been perfected for those patients that are intent on being violent such as drug users and drunks. Once strapped in there's very little threat from them.

We continued with the DI of burns kit, fluids, maternity pack, light rescue equipment, stretcher and finally the carry chair, which is probably the most used bit of kit we carry. I mopped out the back and continued to look under the bonnet, oil, water and then went through the light checks, Blues and conventional. This had already been done by my crewmate but the instructor wanted to see both of us DI both front and back. We went back to the crew room to grab another brew. The DI had taken about 35min, we're only allowed 20mins. This was pointed out and we were told we had to become a lot slicker. Just as the kettle boiled the encoder barked into life,

"Charlie tango one two, (tango indicating a training vehicle) Red call, female collapse"

My heart accelerated and a cold tingle ran up and down my spine. I jumped into the driver's seat. This had been agreed during our DI. As my crewmate wasn't as confident at driving as she was in the attendant's seat. By the same mark I wasn't as confident at attending as I was at driving.

It was now about 0745 and the rush hour traffic was at its worst. We left station and immediately encountered heavy traffic. The two tones were wailing away for all their worth but not everyone heard or saw us. This was the first drive in anger and I wanted it to be smooth but quick. An accident I didn't want. As I threaded the vehicle through the traffic I was mindful of not clipping another vehicle, trying to read the road ahead, not getting blocked in and listening to the instructor who was shouting out the route as it wasn't a location I was familiar with. The vehicle radio sparked-up and started to give us a few more details of what we were going to, so I was taking in information from that as well. My concentration levels went to 100%. At one junction in the centre of town there is a short piece of dual-carriageway before a set of traffic lights. We are not allowed to go on the wrong side of the road because it is a blind junction and other motorists wouldn't see us until too late. The lights were red so we had to stop behind traffic that was already waiting. My thoughts at this time were come on hurry up we've got a collapsed person and this is not helping a time critical problem at all.

In a break from the organised chaos which I had encountered, I noticed that my left foot was shaking on the clutch pedal and I couldn't stop it. I was also feeling quite breathless. I assumed that from the time I had left the station until now I'd probably forgot to breath or I'd been breathing at 100 miles an hour. Either way it was time to control myself and settle down. At last the lights turned green the traffic parted and we were mobile again. This was a great relief to my left leg that was feeling quite weak from all the break dancing it had been doing on the clutch pedal! We finally arrived at the location about 10 minutes after we set out and unsure what to expect. Female collapse was the job description. This could be anything, heart attack, stroke (CVA), epilepsy, faint, drugs overdose, diabetic problems to name a few and the possibility of someone being dead. We grabbed our 1st response bag, which consisted of O2 and resus kit and made our way to the front door. My heart was racing still and now I felt as if my whole body was pulsating with a fearsome blood pressure just from the drive. Now we have a patient to deal with. My crewmate knocked at the front door and shortly after a middle-aged man dressed in nothing but shorts opened the door. "Hello sir did you call for an ambulance"?

"My wife has fallen down the stairs, this way" He beckoned us in and we made our way to his wife who was laid at the bottom of the stairs. There was a tray beside her with a teapot and cups all around as if they had been thrown on the floor. The carpet was steaming from the hot water and milk with sugar mixed into the general mess. She was a slightly built woman in her 40's with a nightdress on. She was unconscious with a cut above her right eye and a pale complexion. My crewmate started her assessment.

"Hello can you hear me"? No reply. She tried a bit of painful stimuli with no effect. I handed my crewmate an O,P airway (a ¼ circle of hollow plastic tube, about 4-5" long, which is placed in the mouth to keep the tongue forward and out of the throat) and I started to get the O2 (god's go gas) sorted out. My crewmate looked at me, "do you want to do this and I'll do the O2" I must of given her a quizzical look because she started to get all sheepish after that. I put the airway in and sat back to let her carry on. She put the O2 on and tried a bit more painful stimuli. Still nothing. I spoke to her husband to try and find out what had gone on.

She had got up to make a cup of tea and the next thing he remembers is a scream and then several bangs. He ran to the top of the stairs and saw her lying at the bottom. He then called us. We did a B/P (blood pressure) that turned out to be low. From this we assumed that she had fainted and fallen down the stairs. From how far up we were unsure.

The O2 therapy was bringing her colour back and generally speaking she was reasonably stable. We applied a cervical spine collar (CX collar) in case of any neck fractures and dressed her head wound which was pretty much superficial, about 3" long and full depth. It would require stitching but that was the least of her worries at the moment. We then set about moving her.

This had to be done with kid gloves. We didn't actually know why she'd fallen in the first place or was she pushed? We didn't know if there was anything more sinister going on, such as a fractured neck, internal injuries or there could have been a cardiac problem. Although only in her 40s it's not unheard of for people in that age category to have heart attacks. We had no means of an ECG machine, that was left up to the hospital to investigate, so we had to consider the worst possible scenario.

As the story unfolded we found out from her husband that she had been prone to faints particularly in the morning. We deduced that she had got up to make a brew and with the combination of her? (Query) low B/P, getting up and being active and then starting to climb the stairs, this could probably of been the trigger for her B/P dropping again. Net result with the body being a fail-safe device, it thought, "no blood to my head must lie down". Unfortunately the body has no concept of what might happen if it lies down straight away! So basically she had fainted from the low BP but had tumbled down X amount of stairs in the process. This in turn caused the head injury. If her head had taken such an impact that had created this laceration there is always the possibility of an underlying problem. Her pupil reaction was good (pupils being the windows to the head) so this could just about rule-out a brain haemorrhage. Also with her BP being low, this would also rule-out a brain haemorrhage. Normally with brain injuries such as CVA (stroke), you would find the BP increasing and the pulse rate decreasing, with a sluggish pupil on the injured side. All these we had ruled out. Good for the patient.

There is no way to rule out a CX (neck) fracture with an unconscious patient. We had to be so careful. The last thing we wanted to do was paralyse her. We collected our scoop stretcher plus straps and strapped her on. It was going to be difficult to move her out of the house as it was small with tight access to the outside. This meant having to make sure she was strapped down securely with no risk of movement.

As we made our way through the house our eyes must have been like saucers. We were extremely worried about the prospect of doing something wrong and causing paralysis to this woman. It was our first day on the road, it was our first job, we had never worked together before and we had an instructor looking over our shoulder at an unconscious patient with a head injury and two very green trainees! As we worked our way through the house with our scoop + patient we came across a 90o corner to the left. My crewmate let the foot end down and I lifted up the head end. Fortunately the patient wasn't heavy and this was easily done with a big grunt and steady movement of the scoop. Slowly we eased her around the corner until we came into open space once again. After a few yards there was another 90o corner to the right. Once again my crewmate lowered her end and I lifted mine. As we turned the corner I had my back and elbows tight against the wall purely because of the amount of room we had to work in. As I eased myself to the left I heard a crash and a shattering of glass. A picture that used to hang on the wall had caught on my shoulder and become unhooked crashing to the ground and breaking. "Sorry about that"

"It's not a problem, my wife is the important one right now"

My forearms were like steel as I was gripping the scoop tightly, so as not to let her go. My muscles in my forearms had all tightened up and this was quite uncomfortable. I was unsure if I was going to be able to make the rest of the route to the ambulance. Finally we were outside in the fresh air with just a short walk to the ambulance. We got her on board and strapped onto the stretcher. We put her onto the main O2 supply, checked her pupil reaction and painful stimuli once again which hadn't changed much. We then organised ourselves for the journey to hospital. The instructor with us said to me "do you mind driving in pink please" This was a new one on me and I must have looked confused.

"Do you know what pink means?"

"No"

"Well when you drive red or 999 you drive with blues and two's going. When you drive normally you drive what we call white. So pink is a mixture of the two. I.e. put your lights on but no noise, we don't want to stress the patient do we?"

I remembered that hearing was the last sense you lose. Just because she was unconscious didn't mean she couldn't hear what was being said or done and the noise from the two tones might have frightened her. Driving on a red call was fine. You rely on the noise of the vehicle to alert motorists that you're behind, or that you're approaching them. But driving without noise was a different ball game. You have to get your nose out early and rely on those coming towards you to move over. The chances are that the motorists you're overtaking don't even know you're there until you're level with them. It takes immense concentration. It must be the most difficult form of driving there is for the ambulance service.

Driving back was a nightmare. I still had the rush hour traffic to contend with and with no noise, added to the complications of driving at speed. An unconscious patient with a head injury in the back, who was not paralysed "yet" but the potential was there and an instructor assessing me. Concentration levels now trying to exceed 100%! About half-a-mile from the hospital is a straight piece of road with a few junctions off it. We were travelling about 50 mph in a 30mph speed limit. I could see a car pulling over to the left to let us through and a car behind him that I still hadn't seen any brake lights from. As I approached them I moved into the middle of the road to overtake. As I went passed the first car I noticed him start to drift over to the right to overtake the car who was pulling over. This I had predicted so I moved over to the right hand lane to avoid a collision. As I drew alongside him he noticed I had blue lights on and started to slow down. A bit late I thought to myself. As I looked up at the road again I noticed a car turning left out of a junction and coming towards me. I checked my mirror and started to pull into the left hand lane. When I looked at the road again a car about 10 meters away had pulled over and stopped for me. Now I had nowhere to go. Curb to my left, oncoming car to my right and a stationary car in front of me.

"BRAKING HARD" I shouted. I covered the brake and eased it on slowly. The brake lights of the car in front were fast approaching. Impact five seconds I thought. The thought of this poor patient in the back, falling down the stairs and lacerating her head, being unconscious and now was going to be involved in an RTA which would probably paralyse her, was horrifying. Impact two seconds I thought and my legs had pins and needles running up and down them as impact was imminent. All of a sudden the car I was about to 'rear end' accelerated away into the space that had been left by the car in front of him which hadn't slowed down at all! I felt relief once again and considered that sometimes it's a blessing when people don't see you! The rest of the journey was completed very carefully with a courteous beep on the horn to the guy who had stopped me burying the ambulance in his rear end.

We arrived at hospital and went into the A+E dept. We started our hand-over which consisted of what had happened, what we had found and the history of the patient. This felt a little intimidating. The nursing staff are excellent and very good at what they do. They knew we were new guys and treated us very gently. A mark of their own professionalism. After moving the patient onto a hospital bed we had a de-brief outside. There was a sarcastic comment about my crewmate not wanting to put an airway in and a brief discussion about moving the stretcher to the front door rather than carrying the patient another 50 yards to the ambulance, good point I thought as I massaged my forearms. There was obvious criticism about not reading the road ahead enough and I should never have put myself in a position where another driver has to bail me out. Apart from that an overall thumbs up was received.

We got back into the vehicle and requested to return to base to re-kit. En-route I caught a reflection of my eyes in the rear view mirror. They were reddened and glazed. Whether this was through lack of sleep or the pressure I had put myself under I didn't know. As I sat in the drivers seat I felt my legs were tired from the driving, my arms were tired from the lifting and I was mentally drained from the thought process we had gone through to try and work out what was wrong with this patient. And this was just a basic faint. What would I feel like after some serious trauma?

For the first time I questioned my mental and physical strength. Still never mind, only another seven hours to go.

Chapter 5

I was now two months into my trainee period and I'd had no real trauma to deal with thus far. I was on a 0800-1600 vehicle that mainly dealt with stretcher cases into the out patient department, clinic appointments and day centre transport. It was designed to give all the guys and girls a break from front line work, one week in 15. Realistically I wanted to be in the thick of it. If there was a 999 (red) call going I wanted to be doing it. The thought of trundling around on non-emergency work all week did not fill me with joy.

It was a dull, wet and grey morning with drizzle still falling. Typical for March in the UK. I was attending and the guy driving was called Brian. Twenty years under his belt and there was nothing he hadn't seen or dealt with in the past. He was a steady bloke and was able to keep up with the ever-changing education that the ambulance service is subjected to. We called clear from the day centre and waited for the next white job (non-emergency) from control.

"Charlie one two I have a red call if you could take details"

"Charlie one two rodger to that send details"

"Could you make your way to the A1304. We have reports of a car Vs a van, reported as trapping over"

"Roger on our way"

We set out from the hospital and I felt a shudder go down my back. This was the first RTA I had been called to where there had been trappings involved. En-route I said to Brian "That's a quick bit of road mate have you had much down there in the past?"

"Oh yes! A lot with nasty injuries and a couple of fatals. When they hit each other on that bit of road, they hit hard!"

"glad I asked!" Brian laughed while my stomach turned over. As we continued our journey the sky got greyer and the drizzle turned into rain. The windscreen of the vehicle was starting to mist up and the roads had become slippery. I put my high-vis jacket on and started to consider what injuries there may be and how I was going to deal with them. The list was endless. Ten to Fifteen minutes later and we arrive on scene. There was a police cordon in place that had been set up to divert traffic away from the incident. He raised his hand to say good morning and lifted the blue and white tape to let us through. At this stage I figured there was going to be some serious injuries. The police don't cordon off a road if they can help it. They would prefer to keep it open.

"Charlie one two in attendance"

When we had visual contact with the scene I noticed another ambulance and a whole mass of fire fighters around the car. As we pulled along side the incident I said to Brian "How on earth do I get amongst that lot?"

"Just push your way in and don't take any grief" The fact he had got all those years of experience in made me feel a lot more confident. I may have the up-to-date knowledge but you can't teach experience or fright and I knew he was hardened to both of them and would look after me. On the other hand I felt frightened and had no experience. I grabbed my resus bag and approached the scene. I was met half way by one of the crew members who was already in attendance and just leaving the scene. He had seen us arrive and got off his vehicle to talk to us. He was a leading Ambulance man (shift Supervisor) from the neighbouring county of Suffolk. He was in his early 30s, tall, laid back with grey hair and glasses. He was softly spoken but each word had an impact that made me listen.

"Hi Ya Chris. We have a car that appears to have aqua-planed, gone across the road and hit the van head-on. The van is fully laden with paper, impact speed about 100mph! We have an infant of about Two years old who has been ejected through the front window of the car and is dead on top of the bank about Five meters in front of the car. We have a child of Seven years old who is unconscious with head injuries and we believe to have a ruptured spleen. We need to get away with him now and get him into theatres. The female driving is the mother of both of them. She is trapped by her legs but conscious and orientated. I'm not sure if she knows if her youngest is dead but from where she is she can see the bundle on the bank. We have covered him/her with a blanket. There are two doctors en-route and their arrival is imminent. Anyway we had better get going, see ya later, good luck!"

"Cheers matey, bye "

As I approached the car there was a mass of yellow helmets. Right Chrissie boy I thought, time to do your stuff. As I arrived at the yellow sea I found myself saying. "Ambulance service excuse me" Elbow, elbow, elbow and found myself on the passenger side of a small blue car. The door was half open and I managed to squeeze the resus bag and me inside the car. Inside the car was somewhat cramped. The engine had pushed the bulkhead and dashboard back about 18" mainly on the drivers side. The dashboard had surrounded the steering wheel and the whole lot was pushed against the driver's chest and abdomen. There was no visual contact with her lower legs as they were covered with metal, plastic and general rubbish that had been thrown around the driver's compartment on impact. I assumed that the pedals had been pushed back and were trapping her lower legs. She had a full depth (down to bone) laceration on her chin about 4" long and another one on her forehead about 5" long also full depth. Some oil had been thrown into the driver's compartment that smelt like burned plastic. The radiator had spilled its contents on to the floor which was steaming and there was the sweet smell of coolant mixed in with the acrid smell of hot oil. The windscreen and driver's side window had smashed and a lot of the glass was now inside the car.

"Hi ya, what's your name then?"

"Jessie" Jessie was about 27 years old. Long black hair and slimly built. Dressed in jeans and an old puffer jacket. She had dried blood over the right side of her face that had seeped out from the forehead laceration. She had a pool of blood on her chest that had been trapped by a crease in her jacket. There was also a slight amount of oil on her face. I figured that it was probably very hot when it first came into contact with her skin.

"Hi ya Jessie, I'm Chris. Sorry to meet you under these circumstances"

"Hi ya Chris" was the answer that came straight back. I was quite taken back. How could she be so polite?

"Well Jessie can you tell me what hurts the most?"

"My right thigh" This was an instant problem as I couldn't see her right thigh.

"OK, anything else hurt at all?" Brian popped his head through the gap that should have been the driver's window.

"All right Chris, anything I can get you?"

"Could I have a cervical collar (Neck splint) please mate"

"No problem" off he went back to the Ambulance that he had turned around and reversed as close as possible to the car.

"Sorry Jessie you were saying?"

"My right thigh and below my knees are stinging like mad" Second problem. I couldn't see her lower legs either. Brian returned with the CX collar "here you go mate"

"Cheers. Jessie what I'm going to do is put a collar around your neck to support your head a little. It's not a fashion accessory and it's not that comfortable but should you have a fracture in your neck it'll support it and stop any further damage." We fitted the collar which was a trial in itself. She had this long hair that kept sticking to the Velcro. We eventually got the collar in a satisfactory position all nice and snug. I checked her pulse which as expected was quicker that normal (Tachycardia). Her breathing rate had gone up to about 35 per min and she was looking a bit grey around the gills.

"Jessie how are you feeling at the moment?"

"Umm not to sure really"

"Do you feel dizzy or nauseas at all?"

"I feel a bit light headed"

"OK what I'm going to do is give you a drop of oxygen. This'll clear your head a bit" I got the O2 on and fitted the mask.

"Jessie its just pure clean air. Just breathe normally for me and let it clear your head mate" The fire service had been beavering away doing their thing. Lots of clonks and bangs had taken place but no real inroads had been achieved to release Jessie.

"Brian you couldn't do me a favour and get the incident officer for me. I would like to start to get Jessie out if we can" Brian returned after a short time with the incident officer and told him "what we need to do is push this dashboard off of Jessie's chest so she can breathe easier and we would also like to get access to her legs and make a further plan from there"

"OK I'll get that sorted out" It hadn't occurred to me at that time, but the reason her breathing had increased was probably due to the dashboard pinning her to the seat and making it difficult for her to inflate her chest fully. Imagine how you would feel with someone sat on your chest for 15-20 minutes. This would also cause the light-headed feeling. Brian must have seen the wheels in my head turning and working it out. I looked at him and he just gave me a big ole Brian smile!

The fire service as requested started to push the dashboard away from Jessie's chest. There was a lot of creaking as the metal bent back on itself and a few loud cracks as the plastic gave way to the strength of the hydraulic rams. This gave Jessie and me the opportunity to have a nervous chuckle together. As one of the loud bangs happened it made me jump. Jessie found this most amusing! She was dead cool!

She had now been trapped for about 35 mins. Whilst she was stable she must have been thinking from time to time about the bundle on top of the bank, as we had moments of a stilted silent atmosphere and I thought she was going to crack on me.

Once her chest was released there was a marked improvement in her breathing and the colour seemed to come back into her cheeks. I tried to look down at her lower legs with my pen torch but the light was minimal and revealed nothing. Brian had already squared the fire service away and knew what my next move 'ought' to be. I looked at him and asked "could you get them to open up the footwell for me?"

"Already in hand Chris" I gave a sigh and rolled my eyes as if to say you flash git.

As the footwell was expanded Jessie started to whimper, "STOP!" I shouted. This was totally out of character for Jessie who had remained composed throughout.

"What's hurting Jessie?"

"My right thigh" I had a quick look at her thigh and it was nearly twice the size of her left. From personal experience I knew what was going on there. As I examined it for a second time, I noticed that her knee had been nipped up either side by a piece of metal from the dashboard that had folded around her patella. As the dashboard was being pushed away from her it was dragging her knee with it and creating the pain in her right thigh. It didn't appear to be penetrating so I thought it could probably be levered out of the way. As I was weighing up the odds another voice said "Hi ya Chris can I do anything to help?" it was one of the doctors.

"Well Phil what we've got is…." I explained all we had found what we had done and the plan of action we were thinking about. "OK I think what I'll do is cannulate (I/V access) and give her some fluids to replace the blood loss and analgesia to ease the discomfort for when we start to move her"

"Sounds good to me" The Doc continued and I explained to Jessie what was going on. I couldn't help noticing that the Doc looked like he had just stepped out of his vegetable patch. There was mud on his hands and he wasn't being too gentle. This flipping great needle went into a vein that made Jessie whimper again. Because the Doc had put the needle in where the elbow bends he needed to also put a splint in place to stop Jessie's arm from bending and creasing the cannula. He used a splint that was nick-named a budgie run. As the name suggests it looked like something you would see in a budgie cage. Made of thick wire it could be bent into the shape of a deformed fracture of the arm, wrist or lower leg etc. Bandaged in place, it makes a good form of immobilisation. This particular time it wasn't the best fitting splint in the world but it was doing the job. The drugs and fluids went in and Jessie was a lot more relaxed.

The fire service released the metal from Jessie's knee and started to expand the footwell. When the time was right I asked them to stop again to allow me the opportunity to have a look at Jessie's lower legs. I shone my pen torch down into the gap about 2" wide and lit up the darkened footwell. I could make out a lot of metalwork and plastic and just managed to light up an area of the floor that revealed a pool of blood that had congealed and was about 1" deep. A smell of raw meat seemed to rise from the footwell. The metalwork of the bulkhead and pedals were now as one. Twisted and contorted by the kinematics of impact. There was some obvious major trauma going on but I was still unable to see exactly what it was with the blood sodden jeans covering the injuries.

I was now able to run my fingers down the front of Jessie's knees and shins. **Her right knee seemed to be intact and her right shin (tibia) was obviously deformed but to what extent I was unsure. There were areas that were soft and areas that offered resistance against my probing fingers, indicating that the tibia was there but was not intact. As I tried to follow the line of her right foot my hand was stopped by a mass of twisted metal. I was unable to get between the back of the lower leg and the seat. I then started to run my fingers down her left leg. Her knee was bleeding and from a rip in her jeans I could see a deep laceration. I used my scissors to open up the damaged area of her jeans to make a better assessment of the injury. After I'd cut a large enough area of the jeans I lifted back the flaps of material to reveal a hole in her leg. The bleeding had stopped and I could see a white/crimson area about 3" in diameter. I looked at the bottom of her thigh from where the injury started to the top of her tibia where the injury finished. The hole was about 1" deep. I could see the base of her femur (thigh bone) and the top of her tibia. There was also the clean whiteness of tendons and ligaments that had once been covered with skin and muscle. These had been exposed when the flesh was ripped from its fixings by the metalwork and plastic of the dashboard. A few bits of ripped fatty tissue were hanging out of the injury where they had once been covered by the patella. The patella was missing. As I ran my fingers down the front of Jessie's tibia it felt like running your fingers over a plastic bag filled with water. There was no resistance to my fingers at all. Again my fingers where stopped from going right down to Jessie's foot by**

twisted metal. I was able to run my fingers down the back of the lower leg and about halfway down I came across a piece of sharp metal that had penetrated right through the leg, front to back.

OK time to re-evaluate what were dealing with.

Airway = Clear

Breathing= Unobstructed

Circulation= We had a circulatory problem due to the haemorrhage from her lower legs and probably from her fractured femur bleeding into her thigh. This was being rectified with fluids which were being administered. So to all intents purposes she was a stable patient. Just the logistical nightmare of getting her out, alive!

Maybe if we could release the clutch pedal from her left leg we could push the dashboard and bulkhead further away and get better access to her legs. I told Jessie I was just leaving for a while to have a chat with my crewmate. I got out of the car and spoke with Brian and the fire service incident officer. I explained that the main problem was that the clutch pedal was impaled in her leg. So every time we move any of the metalwork it was moving her leg and creating pain. Is there anyway of cutting the pedal?

"We've got something called a pedal cutter, it's for cutting pedals funny enough!"

Ok I'm the new boy! How simple would that have been to ask for whilst in the car well I didn't know they carried pedal cutters!

The fire service cut through the pedal, this was painful for Jessie, but I considered this unavoidable and a means to an end. With the clutch pedal cut we continued with rolling the dash and remaining pedals away from Jessie's body. This was done slowly and methodically. Push the dashboard then the pedals, a bit more on the dashboard then the pedals again. Each time only pushing the metalwork away an inch or so. Finally I could get in and make a full assessment of what the injuries were.

I said to Jessie' "I'm going to have a good look at your legs now. If you feel any pain as I run my hands down your legs let me know ok?" Jessie nodded in agreement.

I already knew that her left patella was missing and I thought that her right femur was fractured. I started once again with the right leg. Her femur was still twice the size of her left. I placed my hand just below her right hip and the other on the inside of her lower thigh. By applying gentle pressure there was a feeling of bones grinding together and a jerk from Jessie. This confirmed what I had thought, fractured femur. I was now able to cut away the jeans from her lower right leg.

As I looked I could see that the flesh was intact with some lacerations on the front of her shin. Midway down her lower leg it was bent at an angle of 45o or so, indicating that her Tib and Fib were both fractured. I cut off her sandal to have a better look at her right foot. Her foot was virtually intact but had the Little toe and the fourth toe missing. In the footwell of the car was a mass of congealed blood that stank of raw meat with the toes amongst the plastic and metal that had broken loose. I picked up the toes and gave them to Brian. I wasn't sure if they could be salvaged or not.

I now turned my attentions to Jessie's lower left leg. As I cut the trouser leg away I was confronted with a mass of meat basically. Her flesh had been stripped from the bone. The pedal in turn had shattered the bone as it went through. There were fragments of bone all over the floor. Some tiny bits and some about 1" in size. I figured these were unsalvageable. Her leg laid open as if it had been hit with a machete, from just below her knee to the top of her foot. I could see the muscles, tendons and ligaments that had all been pulled off their fixings and hung aimlessly with the rest of the ripped flesh. Her foot was pulp, semi submerged in the pool of blood and looked like a punnet of mince. Beside it lay the white disk shaped patella.

All of my observations out of the way, it was time to get Jessie out of the car. I realised that there had been a lot of cutting and banging going on but was unsure why. I looked at Brian "we need to get her out soonest really mate"

"I've got the fire service to cut the roof off and we can lift her out onto our scoop stretcher, strap her down and move her into the ambulance". I was so relieved. I had no idea how we were going to move her but as usual Brian was one step ahead of the game.

"Jessie the roof's going to come off of your car and were going to lift you out and onto a stretcher we have waiting. There's going to be a lot of yap going on between us and the fire service, just go with it Jessie and we'll have you out and a lot more comfortable very soon" Jessie being whacked out on morphine just nodded her head.

The roof came of in a matter of minutes and the kit was ready and waiting. Brian recruited some fire service personnel and between us we all lifted Jessie clear of the wreck. It was my job to cradle the injured lower legs. As Jessie was in the sitting position we were unable to get any form of splints in place. This unfortunately left her legs with no support. As Jessie came out of the vehicle I tried to keep everything as in-line as possible.

I managed to get my hands under Jessie's knees and as she was lifted out of the seat I was able to straighten her legs and get my forearms under what was left of her lower legs. I locked her feet against my chest to keep everything in place, to stop it all flailing around. I noticed a warm feeling running down both arms. Needless to say that with all the injuries Jessie had received and being unable to dress her wounds the blood was flowing considerably. Most of which trickled down the inside of the arms of my Hi-Vis jacket, warm as it was but not particularly pleasant!

We strapped her to the scoop stretcher, loosely covering her wounds and moved her into the Ambulance. When we got Jessie into the ambulance I tried to manipulate her lower legs so if nothing else they looked like lower legs. I cupped my hands either side of her left calf-muscles and basically tried to mould what tissue there was into the shape of what a calf-muscle and lower leg should look like. However, as well as this looked, as soon as I released the support I was giving to the muscle and remaining tissue, it became obvious that my efforts were futile. With very little skeletal support, muscle tone absent and the lack of flesh, all the tissue laid flat on the stretcher. We managed to put a leg splint in situ and pack it with various dressings and bandages to keep the tissues as close knit as possible to try and salvage some form of oxygenation for the remaining tissue etc.

With pain relief administered, fluids up and running, legs splinted and Jessie secure on the stretcher it was time to role to the local Hospital. The journey in with a patient (PT) in Jessie's condition always seems to take longer than anticipated. There is nothing else to do but sit back and talk. But with Jessie now full of morphine this wasn't an option. I just had to sit back and make sure the morphine didn't create a respiratory problem and wait for the arrival at the Hospital. We handed Jessie over to the A/E staff and then returned to base to re-kit and grab a brew.

We had done a couple of other jobs since taking Jessie in and had landed up at A/E once again. I asked one of the nurses, who we had handed over to, how Jessie was doing.

"Not too bad. We're waiting for a theatre bed to become available so we can amputate her lower left leg. We've just been able to get hold of her husband. He's on his way in now"

This hit me harder than turning up at the scene. Hubby has gone to work this morning with 2 kids and an extremely stoic wife at home. He is about to be told he has 1 dead child, 1 that is on the critical list and a wife that won't walk properly again,

How's your luck?

Chapter 6

I was now five years into my service and I'd had my fair share of both trauma and medical emergencies. The title of paramedic was now being bounced around in the press on a daily basis. Mainly due to Ken Clarke trying to screw us over for money and creating the national Ambulance dispute over Christmas and the New Year 1989-1990. It was Paramedics this and Paramedics that. Although to us in the service it was just a new title and we had hardly any Paramedics at all. A few staff had gone away with a lot failing and the remainder were so stressed out. One bloke on the course even had a heart attack whilst on the course, suppose he was in one of the best places though!!

Not being one to be fazed to easy and I always like a challenge. I put my name forward for the paramedic course entrance exam that we have to pass before being accepted onto the course. I started reading books galore trying to educate myself. I'm no academic and have to work hard at reading, I just find it boring really. Show me a practical skill once and it'll stay with me forever. Give me a book to read and I'll have to read it three times before I can understand what it's on about. I had about two months to inwardly digest all the information I was reading. Slack times at work, late nights and days off were all used for reading, it became all-consuming. But the way I saw it, it was a lot of reading and theory to achieve practical skills.

All theoried up and it was the big day. The exams consisted of 40 Mcq's (multi-choice questions) and 40 true/false questions. Also five short essays had to be completed which are taken from a list of 10 headings. All the questions were relevant to either patient care or anatomy and physiology, as an example:- Describe your assessment, diagnosis and treatment of a patient who you believe to be suffering with a myocardial infarction (heart attack). Or something like:- draw a NSR (normal sinus rhythm) ECG and describe what is happening to the heart at each particular part of the ECG, how much time is allowed for each part movement of the heart under normal circumstances. Confused? I won't either confuse or bore you with any more, but that'll give you a brief insight as to what was expected and that was just to get onto the bloody course! All in all the exams took about six hours. I didn't feel particularly confident with my answers but then we were all doubting ourselves and at the end of it we were all knackered. For those who passed this stage there are some further practical exams to be done. These are things like CPR working with a de-fib (shock box) of which nothing less than the usual 100% was acceptable. We would also be examined on conscious and unconscious patient assessment and just for good measure a couple of trauma scenarios just to ensure you were completely mentally drained.

About two weeks later the results arrived on my doormat. I sat down with a brew and opened the letter, I had failed. The pass mark for the MCQ and T/F questions was 80%. The service uses a negative marking system, so basically you get a 1.25% for each question you get right. Nothing for those you leave unanswered but the killer is each question you get wrong they'll deduct 1.25%! The mistake I had made was taking a stab at a couple of questions I didn't know the answers to and getting them wrong. So after the 5% had been deducted from my correct answers it left me with 77.5%. Pissed off I certainly was. If only I had left them alone. Still lesson learned, if in doubt, leave it alone.

A bit battered from my first entrance exam failure and the same going on in my personal life, it was some 12 months before I sat the entrance exam again. This time I felt a lot more confident. I'd got another 12 months of 'on the road experience' and I'd had another 12 months to consolidate and understand what I had read in all those books. Also the rules for marking the exams had changed. Instead of using the torturous negative marking system the service had gone back to a marking system that normal people use! I.e. 1 mark for each correct answer and nothing for leaving or getting an answer wrong, simple or what? No! What they decided to do, so as not to make it to easy, was to increase the pass mark from 80% to 85%, great! However I knuckled down again and re-sat the exam. This time I was successful and passed with plenty to spare. The practical scenarios have never really fazed me too much. A few butterflies beforehand but as soon as I get into the swing of my questioning they are soon forgotten. With all the various entrance exams passed and out of the way I was accepted onto the paramedic course proper.

In the two months leading up to the paramedic course once again my life revolved around reading, reading and more reading. The course itself was split into three stages.

Stage 1:- anatomy and physiology going into quite significant depth. This lasts for one week then back on the following Monday for two days of exams. If on Tuesday afternoon you have failed you're thrown off of the course and can't return until you've done all the entrance exams again.

Stage 2:- lasts for four weeks and it's learning about *fluid therapy, cannulation intra-venous access* (this is where you put a needle into a vein and secure it in place. This allows fluids and drugs to be administered straight into the circulatory system. (Putting an IV up as they say in all the films!).

Intubating, (this is where a tube is passed through the vocal cords and into the airway. This is also secured into place by means of a small inflatable balloon at the base of intubation tube. This allows oxygen to be passed straight into the lungs by way of ventilating).

Drugs and drug therapy, the drugs which we carry on the ambulances all have their own effects, side-effects and dosages. These all have to be learnt and recalled without hesitation.

ECG recognition. Interpret what that wiggly line really means on the De-fib screen in a lot more depth than we had been previously taught. And to know what drugs would be applicable to rectify a cardiac condition that has been recognised. This stage of the course also went a lot deeper into how various illnesses, injuries and drugs affect other parts of the body. The list is long and could be mind boggling, so let's leave it at that!

Stage 3:- was a lot more laid back. five weeks in a warm hospital.

One week on the coronary care unit. Two weeks in operating theatre and Two weeks putting it all together in the Accident and Emergency dept (A&E), working with the casualties as they come through the doors. There would be a final Interview with the head of the A+E department, talking through a couple of scenarios. But first the course has to be passed.

Stage 1
Day 1. Twelve of us started the course. We spent all day studying the 'Nervous System'. It's a bit like being taught about your house electrics all in one day, it's complicated! It was eight hours of constant banging on

about efferent nerves and afferent nerves, spinal synapses the autonomic nervous system, parasympathetic and sympathetic nervous systems, nerves which are under control of our will and those which are not. Needless to say by 6pm we were all mentally knackered! You could look into each other's eyes and see a misty redness instead of the white of the eye. Guy's and gal's all under pressure from day one. After tea we done what all good Guy's and Gal's do when they're on a course, hit the bar! And the topic of conversation? 'The Nervous System'!! As anoraky as it seems I think I probably learnt as much in the bar each night as I did in the lessons. At some point through the evening after swallowing one or two pints of the golden nectar, one of the instructors informed us that we had a one-hour confirmation paper (exam about the previous days tuition) in the morning about the nervous system. Great! Most of us vacated the bar at this point, complete with pints and did a bit more reading before hitting the sack.

The following morning as sure as night follows day we had our confirmation paper, 60mcq's and two short essay questions. Then called into the office for a blow-by-blow account of how well or how badly we had done. If we weren't above the standard then extra studying would be given out, along with another confirmation paper to be sat the following day, after we had grabbed a short dinner break. This would obviously eat into study time allowed for that day's tuition and the following days confirmation paper. This would inevitably mean either falling behind or working late into the night. Neither of which were a good idea.

By 10am on day two after the confirmation paper we all felt mentally drained. Once again lots of misty red eyes walking around. After the conformation paper we spent all day studying 'the cardio-vascular system'. That evening into the bar and the following morning a one-hour confirmation paper before spending day three studying the 'respiratory System' and then the following day a confirmation paper. This continued for the week. We had the weekend off and then back on Monday and Tuesday for two days of exams about stuff we had learned the previous week. This was the first real crunch time. The confirmation papers were not 'pass or fail' but the instructors kept on at you like a dog with a bone until you reached above the standard that was required to pass the course. The theory being that if you knew more than was needed you could afford to forget some. If we were to fail now we would be thrown off the course.

The two days were relentless. From 9am to midday were Mcq's and short essay questions. No one was allowed to talk about the answers they had given as this may lead someone to think they had failed at the first stage and not give 100% for the next part. When, in reality, it could be the other person that had failed. We stopped for dinner and in the afternoon we then had practical scenarios to go through. The practical scenarios had a pass mark of 100%. On the Tuesday we had more Mcq's to start with, until 11am, then more practical's until 1pm, followed by a quick late lunch. After lunch there had been some time set aside for anyone who hadn't quite reached the standard to re-take the practical scenarios. This was not an option for the written papers. Four people were called in one at a time which left the rest of us sitting around in the seminar room in silent solitude. After about five minutes the door opened and the course co-ordinator came in.

"Well ladies and gentlemen I'm sorry to say that you will all have to come back in the future" Thoughts of going back and having to re-study wasn't filling me with to much happiness. All those bloody confirmation papers to sit again.

"Unfortunately you're all through to the second stage of the course, well done".

Git! It took a second to register what he had said but we had all passed stage one.

"Enjoy the rest of your week off and see you back here on Monday. Hopefully for four weeks and we can get stuck in to some real Paramedic Techniques!"

Stage 2

This stage of the course is a lot more enjoyable. We are now dealing with the more practical aspects of canulating, Intubating, fluids, drugs and de-fibrillating. There is still a lot of theory to be learnt and exams to be sat. But it's a lot more laid-back and we now have something to relate to.

We all had to draw a number out of a hat. This is now our candidate number. These numbers went at the top of the exam papers to give us anonymity. This is so the instructors, when marking papers, would not be able to have their favourites! Yeah right! There's only eight of us left on the course. Of course the instructors won't remember who is which number! I drew out number five. There was a film around at the time called 'Short Circuit' it was a loveable, military robot that had been accidentally electrocuted, went bonkers and became almost human-like, with feelings and a sense of understanding. It had number 5 printed on the back of its head and as a result was called 'number 5'. The MOD wanted to take it apart due to the technology within it. When the robot heard and understood what 'disassemble' meant it kept banging on about 'number 5 stay alive, number 5 stay alive, no disassemble!' So I was safe in the knowledge that number 5 would probably stay alive! Well we all look for some form of inspiration in times of need!

There was still a lot of learning that went on in the bar of an evening but a lot of what we were doing now was practical and we couldn't bring the bar to the accommodation, but we could take the various manikins, arms (for cannulation), heads (for intubation) and ECG machines to the bar. We did get some strange looks! One night after two weeks of being on the course, a good friend of mine called John and me decided not go to the bar as we wanted to learn to read ECG's. Not just to read them but to be slick at reading them. We set ourselves up in his room with a self test machine and a de-fib. Just after our evening meal we started to go through the ECG's working the system the service had taught us. This continued until 3am, both of us were chin-strapped but time well spent. By this time we could give each other an ECG and within five or six seconds of it appearing on the 3" screen we had worked out what the problem was and what drugs would be required to rectify it. This was a total confidence boost for the pair of us. ECG recognition can be complicated and is one of the more difficult and important aspects of pre-hospital diagnosis and we had cracked it. It made me feel that maybe good ole number 5 was going to stay alive till the end of the course!

During the course we had guest speakers come in and give talks about their specialist subjects. For instance a chest surgeon talked about how various stab injuries would affect breathing, what signs and symptoms we would find from being stabbed in various places. For example, if someone was stabbed just below the ribs they may complain about having shoulder tip pain. Totally unrelated you may think? Being stabbed just under the ribs and combined with shoulder tip pain is quite significant. Because of the way the nervous system is formed and how the nerves run, the shoulder tip pain is an indication that the diaphragm could be lacerated and as a result the patients breathing will become worse. As the diaphragm stretches with each intake of breath, the lacerated area will become greater. Net result if gone untreated? - Probably death! So no messing around on scene with the patient as he/she needs to be in the operating theatre ASAP. Another speaker we had gave us a talk about blast injuries, and how, not only does the outer flesh become obviously burnt and lacerated but how internal organs can become ruptured. Because of the vast pressure-increase which happens during an explosion, the pressure within the body cavity also increases. The hollow organs such as liver, lungs, kidneys 'oh' and of course the heart (I knew there was another important one!) will become over-inflated and may burst. Whilst patients may die immediately with big explosions with smaller explosions, like a gallon of petrol or a gas cylinder, they may well survive initially. But we had to be aware that internal haemorrhages will probably be present and we need to intervene quickly to prevent the casualty from bleeding to death internally or dying from shock. Both of which would be treated with I/V Fluids and a high concentration of Oxygen. Another speaker spoke about Maxilla Facial Injuries. This is a description of how the facial bones fracture on impact. Some of the photos were pretty gruesome of people that had gone through windscreens or had been hit with a blunt weapon such as a baseball bat. But it seemed that the face fractures in three different but regular ways, depending on how much force it has been subjected to. Obviously the greater the force the worse the fracture. Apparently some Guy called Le-Forte found this out by getting hold of some second-hand skulls! Laying them face up on the floor and dropping bricks on them from various heights. He found that the skull had weak points in it and would regularly fracture in the same three places which could be easily repaired! I think this particular experiment took place well before music, dancehalls, discos or night clubs were invented. I take it, it was a good night in! Well I found it fascinating!

The final week of stage two is allocated for revision and final exams. I wasn't too fazed by the practical exams but the theory I had my concerns about. We had taken on board a lot of information from the various reference books we had to study from and my hand written course notes now filled a four ringed lever arch file! The huge question was: Is number 5 going to be disassembled or live to tell the tale? The week went past pretty quickly as you would expect. We all went through extreme emotions. Coming out of one exam feeling very confident and coming out of another feeling we had blown it. This was applicable to everybody on the course without exception. I came out of one of the short answer essay exams (mainly about chemistry) and felt I'd totally lost the plot. The two hours that we were in the exam room seemed to go on forever. When I came out I felt I'd missed so much information that the examiner would want to see. When I got back to my room I checked through my notes and sure enough there was a lot I had missed but there was quite a bit that I had got down as well. I figured this was my stumbling block and I was confident this paper was going to cost me the course. I was so pissed off with myself that I got smashed in the bar that night! A lot of bonding went on in the final week, particularly in the bar! All exams out of the way and it was crunch time. When our number was called out we went into a room, told the results and left the room via another door, this led down a short corridor to the training department coffee room. If we had failed it gave us the opportunity to leave the grounds, go walk about and gather our thoughts before having to face up to the rest of the course. Not that there would have been any ridiculing but you were going to be pretty upset.

"Number one" called the instructor, in went number one. About 10 minutes went past and we heard the other door open and close. About two minutes later the instructor came into our room "number two" in went number two. After about five mins we heard this scream and wailing and then the outside door, BANG! We all correctly assumed that number two had failed. "Number 3" in he went 10 minutes later we heard the outside door "Number 4" and in she went. My turn next, it felt as if my whole chest was trying to erupt inside. I felt my breathing increase and my pulse was speedily bouncing along. My palms were sweaty and my legs felt heavy from pins and needles. "Ooer, I hope they hurry up" I muttered out loud. The ten minutes felt like a lifetime. Finally we heard the outside door open and close. I physically felt sick. The instructor didn't arrive as quickly as I'd expected. Got to be trouble I thought. After what seemed like an eternity he opened the door "Number 5". It felt like I was walking to the Gallows. When I got into the room there was the chief instructor the course co-ordinator, the personnel manager and my tutor.

"Sit down Chris, well how do you feel you got on then?"

I explained that I felt the practical assessments went ok but I was unsure about the theory exams and mainly the short answer essay that I felt I'd blown. He smiled and ignored my comment, my heart sank. That was clearly not a good sign. He went on to ask me how I felt the course was run and any comments I had so they could improve the course for the future etc. I was thinking, bloody hell mate just give me the poxy result and get me out of here. After we had done the talky thing finally he said "OK Chris lets take a look at your results" and he cast his eyes over my results summary sheet, kind of umm'ing as he went.

"Can you remember what the pass marks are for the written answers?"

"85%"

"That's correct, take a look at this" he turned the summary sheet towards me. I couldn't make head nor tail about what result related to which exam. I was frantically looking for the chemistry paper result. He must have seen the desperation in my face. He took the summary sheet away and said "is there anything particular you are looking for?"

"Yes, the chemistry result".

"You mean this one" and pointed to a % result. 85%.

"Well done Chris, I'm pleased to tell you, you have passed. But it was a close run thing!" He shook my hand. I punched the air and unfortunately for him I squeezed my right hand all at the same time. I've got quite a strong grip and him being a pen pusher wasn't used to having his hand held quite as tight!! He let out a little squeal and ouch! "Oops sorry about that" I said and released my grip. Too late I thought you've already passed me! We all eventually met up and it turned out that three more had failed. I felt pretty bad for the guys and gals who had failed as they had been to hell and back and must have felt that it was all for nothing.

There were five of us in the vehicle which took us back to our various stations around the area that evening. Two of the guys who had failed were with us. I'd got a couple of beers in my bag that I'd been keeping for the journey home to celebrate if I had successfully completed the course. But under the circumstances they stayed in my bag. About half way home we came across an RTA, we pulled over and all de-bussed. Shortly after the A&E crew arrived on scene. There were no real injuries just cuts and bruises. But it was quite amusing having seven of us on scene at one time. It must have looked to the general public as if there was something major happening. It was such a relief to get home. Mum and Dad were both there and I gave them the good news. Mum did her usual and disappeared into the kitchen, food! I opened my bag, handed Dad a beer and cracked one open myself, "thank God that's over. Pub tonight?"

Stage 3

I had been looking forward to the third Stage of the course as its purely practical skills, working on live patients, well at least they were before I got my hands on them! The first part is in the coronary care dept. More tests are undertaken and signatures have to be collected from the coronary care staff to say that you are competent at various tasks. Mainly down to ECG recognition and drug treatment/therapy of cardiac conditions. The second part was two weeks in the operating theatres. Cannulating and Intubating patients as they are knocked out by anaesthetists. This is very closely watched by the anaesthetists and if any major complications arise you're thrown off the unit. Once again paperwork has to be signed by the anaesthetists to say that you're competent at the skills performed. This part

I found a really interesting time. I'm one of those people who likes to know how things work. I get it from my Dad who used to be an aircraft inspector. When you're gazing into an abdominal cavity or a knee joint that's been opened up there's a whole lot of, "what's this do" and "what's that bit there?" all in all I was a complete pain in the arse to the surgeons but there was some serious anatomy and physiology to be learned. As a result of my intrigue and curiosity I had to have the two weeks extended for a further two days to get all my signatures. The third and final placement was for two weeks in the A/E Dept. This is where you pull it all together. Dealing with victims who have had heart attacks, fractured bones, dog bites, RTA's etc, you know what I'm talking about. You get attached to a senior Nurse (nice!) and they'll watch you assess and treat patients as they come through the doors. If it's anything that's serious then you work with the A/E consultant and he or she will quiz you about decisions you're making and why, and what treatment you'll be giving and why. Whilst it's designed to put you under pressure you don't feel it at the time as your dialling in on what you're doing and trying to think two steps ahead. The worst part is the waiting when crews have alerted A/E that they'll be arriving with a patient in ten mins or so, and have given a sit-rep (situation report) of what they're coming in with. Again this part I thoroughly enjoyed. Always in the back of your mind your thinking that if it all goes to rat shit then there's someone there to bail you out. Albeit it would be considered a failure.

With the three placements completed and all signatures in the boxes the very last part is an interview with the head of A/E and my instructor. I was given two scenarios. The first one I was called to a curry house the other side of town where someone had collapsed. As I was going through my assessment of the patient it became obvious that he was a diabetic that had gone hypo, probably due to alcohol consumption. Treatment being a quick I/V slug of 50% glucose, which is like treacle and you need the grip of an ape to get it through the cannula. Keep a watchful eye in case he vomits, bearing in mind he'd consumed a lot of alcohol on top of a vindaloo, and compromises his airway. Wait for him to come to, which is very quick when using glucose and off to hospital should he decide to have another Hypo. 'That was simple enough' I thought 'the complicated one is coming next'. This scenario was where someone has been stabbed in the Abdomen at a location about one minute's drive from the hospital. When I arrive I find a male who is pale, sweaty and is lying in a pool of blood. My action was simple. Plug the hole and whip him to the hospital soonest. My thoughts were that although I could put a line up and squeeze lots of fluid into him, ultimately he needs to be in theatres, opened up and have the deeper wounds stitched first. Definitive care being the only option for survival. That wasn't too bad either I thought.

About an hour had past and both scenarios dealt with. My instructor and the A/E consultant looked at each other and humorously discussed between themselves should we let him loose on the unsuspecting public? Umm not sure about that! My instructor looked at me "what do you reckon then Chris"?

"Too bloody right!"

He lent forward and shook my hand "well done Chris, how do you feel?"

"Exhausted"

I was now up and running as a Paramedic, frightening!

Chapter 7

I had a well-earned break over the weekend and it was back to work 0800 Monday morning. I was lucky enough to be crewed with another Paramedic called Steve whom I had plenty of respect for both professionally and socially. Steve had qualified about 12 months previous. He'd gone away on the course I would have gone on if I'd passed my first entrance exam. We DI'd (daily inspection) the vehicle and during this time we discussed our plan of attack. I was going to kick the job off and if I wound up getting stuck or cocking things up he would take over. Just as we finished our DI the encoder went off,

"Charlie Zero Three Red call (999) to blar, blar, blar. We have two midwives on scene who have been present at a home delivery. They are requesting a Paramedic crew, for what reason we still don't know over"

"Charlie Zero Three all received" we booked onto the job and off we went. It felt like my stomach was falling out of my arse! A bit like the feeling us guys get when you're going to ask your first girlfriend out! Needless to say that given the time of day the traffic was its usual rush hour heavy self and we seemed to be making slow progress. I sat in the attendant's seat thinking, c'mon Steve get your boot down. Although he was driving as quick as the traffic would allow him.

"Control to Charlie Zero Three"

"Charlie Zero Three go ahead"

"Charlie Zero Three. Apparently the patient has developed a serious haemorrhage during childbirth and is now very hypotensive (Low Blood Pressure). *We believe they want you there for fluid replacement, over"*

Oops there goes the belly again!

"Charlie Zero Three, thanks for the info, all received, over"

A few minutes later we arrived at the location. We walked into the house and heard some voices upstairs. We made our way up to find out what was going on. We walked into a bedroom and introduced ourselves. There were two midwives who were knelt beside the bed. The baby was wrapped up in the usual blankets to keep it warm, it's little crumpled up face the only part visible to the outside world to which it had become a part of. The bed sheets, although placed back over the patient were obviously blood sodden. I cast my eyes towards the new mum. She looked as if she had run a marathon. Very pale and extremely sweaty. I took her wrist to take a pulse, this was absent. One of the midwives started to give me a hand-over. She also informed me that her sidekick was a trainee and was interested in watching what us Paramedics are capable of! There goes the belly again. The mid-wife finished off by saying what the patient needed was fluid replacement. No shit Sherlock, kinda worked that one out for myself but I kept it to myself.

I placed and tightened my tourniquet on the patient's upper arm and waited for a vein to show itself so I could cannulate. Unfortunately due to her low BP she was badly shut down (limited circulation to her extremities) and her veins had become very small and skinny. What I needed was a klonking great vein to get a big bore needle into her so I could administer fluids ASAP. The other point was that she was still haemorrhaging quite severely and needed to be in the operating theatres for surgery. It's all very well pumping loads of fluids into someone but as I've said before, definitive care is what they need.

So the situation. Mum is as sick as a hangover and is bleeding out like a busted water main. As a result any veins in her arms have been reduced to no more than empty flat pipe work. There's a trainee mid-wife who's watching me like a hawk as she's interested in what us Paramedics are capable of. Steve is looking over my shoulder to make sure all goes well and this my first on the road cannulation. Blimey, it couldn't have got any easier!! Well Chrissie-boy, time to do your stuff again.

"Can I have a 16gauge cannula please" (medium sized)

"A 16gauge, err hold on a moment matey" Steve rummaged through the cannulation tray. There were needles falling all over the floor, the lid came off of it's hinges. Finally Steve said "Ah! Got one" He then struggled to get the packaging open and with a big ole heave-ho ripped the base away from the rest of the packaging. The needle came flying out and landed on the floor about three feet away. Steve rummaged for another cannula, pulled the packaging away as normal and handed me the cannula. I felt a little cold sweat breaking out over my forehead as I lined up the point of the needle with the pale blue thready vein. As I pushed the point into the patient she tensed up from the burning sensation I was inflicting on her. I could hear my own heartbeat as the pressure grew on me and the situation got to the point of, is it in or have I loused it up? As I advanced the needle I got a flash back in the head of the cannula. (confirmation that the cannula was in the vein) All I had to do now was advance the cannula nice and smooth following the contours of the vein, so not to push the cannula through the other side of the vein creating a small internal bleed of her arm. She'd got enough bleeding going on already! The cannula was fully advanced with no apparent mistakes. Steve went to hand me a cannula dressing to anchor the cannula in place.

"Can I have a flush please Steve" Steve looked at me for a moment. You could see the cogs of his brain turning over then the realisation of his mistake hit home "Oops sorry matey" No point anchoring it in place if it's not going to work properly. The standard procedure is to run a small amount of sterile water through the cannula first to further confirm its placement. Steve once again rummaged through the by now bomb damaged cannulation tray "Here we are" he found an ampoule of sterile water (flush) and a 5ml syringe. As he was drawing the flush into the syringe somehow the ampoule came adrift, flew through the air and landed next to the cannula that had done the same thing earlier. "Be with ya in a minute Chris" Another quick rummage and Steve was drawing up another flush which he then handed to me. As I pushed the fluid into the cannula it went through with no resistance and no ballooning of the area. Another confirmation that the cannulation was successful. Once I'd flushed the cannula Steve handed me the already prepared cannula dressing. I anchored the cannula in place "have you got the fluids mate?"

"Ah, no but I will have in a minute" Steve got the fluids run through in his usual efficient manner and handed me the giving set which I attached to the cannula. I opened up the valve and started the fluids running at a pretty quick rate. Ultimately we needed to get Mum moved to the Theatres. However to try this straight away would have been foolish. I figured that if we had tried to move her at the moment with no radial pulses, she would have probably fainted or at very least felt faint and nauseous. We explained to all who were present what our intentions were and played the waiting game. After 10mins or so of the fluids going in I checked her radial pulse again, they had now returned. I took another BP which indicated that the fluids were doing their job. I now slowed the fluid administration down by shutting the valve off slightly.

We got Mum onto our carry chair and carried her down the stairs and into the Ambulance. Once we had got her comfortable I checked her BP once again. This was now at a much more acceptable level. I set the fluids to run at a rate that would hopefully maintain her BP. This can only be done if you're putting the fluids in at the same speed as she is losing blood. Although she was a lot more stable now she was still bleeding.

The thing with fluid replacement is that it's not just a case of putting a line in and letting the fluids run too quickly. With pre-hospital care, research has shown that if the fluids go in too quickly and the BP gets raised too high, you run the risk of knocking off the very delicate clots that may have already formed at the injury site. This in turn would increase the bleeding and you wind up with a less stable casualty than you started with. By the same mark if you don't administer the fluids quick enough the bleed outweighs the fluid replacement, the BP drops and once again you wind up with an unstable casualty. So it's a question of monitoring your patient and making adjustments as necessary.

The journey into hospital was trouble-free and we got Mum onto the ward in a far better state than when we arrived at her bedside. However she almost certainly would need some form of surgical intervention to rectify the problem.

Steve and myself, when we got outside of the maternity unit, just buckled up from laughter. Steve was saying that he'd now had enough of being a Paramedic helper as it was more difficult than doing the skills themselves. From my point of view I asked Steve to keep his juggling tricks for when he was at home entertaining the family, although it made a good ice-breaker for me. All in all the job went well and we had achieved our aim.

Chapter 8

A few months later, on a nice sunny day we were activated to a single m/cycle RTA. On our arrival there was a big burly biker laid on the ground chatting to the police. It looked as if he had come from the exit of a round-about a bit quick and had run out of road. He had skidded on the road for a while, then onto a flat grass verge which was about 10 feet in width and tree lined. It looked as if he had laid the bike down on its right side. When I got to his side I introduced myself and asked his name "Tuscan" was the reply.

"Morning Tuscan, how ya feeling?"

"My right knee" as I looked towards his right knee there was an obvious tear in his jeans but it didn't look like there was too much damage going on. I went through my usual primary and secondary survey and finally arrived at his damaged right knee.

"Right Tuscan I'm going to cut your jeans to have a better look, is that ok?"

"Yes but be careful"

"No problem" as I cut his jeans he let out a huge ARRRRHHH

"What's the problem Tuscan?"

"My knee! My Knee!

"But I haven't touched it yet!"

"I know but I'm expecting it to hurt"

"Well give me a chance to get close to you Tuscan. You never know it may not hurt. You frightened the bloody life out of me."

"Ok I'm sorry"

"Shall we try again?"

"Ok but be careful"

"Given a chance and I will be" I gently cut his jeans away from his knee to expose what ever was going on underneath. When I looked at his knee there was a graze over his patella but the patella all looked in tact.

"Tuscan I'm going to touch your knee is that ok?"

"If you must"

"Well I'd like to find out what's going on mate"

"Ok but steady" as I moved my fingers towards his knee "ARRRRH-HH"

"Tuscan I haven't touched you yet"

"I know I know but I know it's going to hurt"

"Right-e-o Tuscan. Now what I'm going to do is gently touch the outside of your knee" as my glove made contact with his skin "ARRRRH-HH"

"What's hurting Tuscan?"

"The top of my knee"

"But I was touching the outside of your knee not the top of it"

"I know but I know its going to hurt" Blimey I thought we're getting nowhere very fast here. I looked towards my crewmate "could you get me a leg splint please" I rolled my eyes as if to say bloody wimp "we'll treat it as if it's fractured but I'm not convinced". Tuscan sparked into life once again

"Fractured, fractured you think my leg is fractured?"

"No Tuscan, I don't think your leg is fractured but I can't get close enough to have a good look can I!"

"Oh no I've fractured my leg, will it fix ok?"

No Tuscan I don't think you've fractured your leg"

"But you said it was fractured"

"No, I said we will treat it as if it's fractured but I'm not convinced"

With a lot more ARRRRHHH's from Tuscan we finally got his leg in a splint and Tuscan into the ambulance. En-route I wanted to put a probe on his finger. It's called a pulse oximeter. It's basically a peg with a lightweight spring and an infrared light recessed into a foam lining. It has a pick up on one side and on the other side, it has an infra-red light which shines a light through the finger. As the name suggests, it takes your pulse and measures the oxygen within the blood. It's an extremely helpful guide when dealing with respiratory illnesses, chest injuries and cardiac cases. These could all potentially lower the oxygen saturation of the blood. You also get the standard issue bleep each time the heart beats.

So without looking at it you can keep a mental tally of any changing heart rate.

I said to Tuscan "could you take your glove off please/"

"No!"

"Why not?"

"Safety!"

"Safety?"

"Yes safety"

"What do you mean safety?"

"Safety, in case we crash!"

"Now Tuscan" I lent forward towards Tuscan who was lying on the opposite stretcher "We're in a big van that is covered in green and yellow Hi-Vis squares. The guy driving has been through and passed an extended driving course. You're strapped on a stretcher that is secured to the sidewall of the vehicle by a steel framework! You are possibly as safe as you can be whilst donning decent tarmac in the UK! Please can you take off your glove?" I was now getting very peeved with Tuscan!

"Why what are you going to do?"

"I would like to put this probe on you're finger"

"What does it do?"

"It just takes your pulse and a couple of other readings"

"How does it do that?" I figured it was time that I had a bit of fun with Tuscan.

"Well Tuscan, this little peg goes over your finger and two needles shoot out, one from either side of the peg. one buries itself into your nail bed and the other from the opposite side goes through you skin. They both meet in the middle of the bone and measure the pulse rate and oxygen saturation of your blood" Tuscan' face was a picture. His mouth dropped open, his face went bright red and his eyes were the size of a dinner plate. He buried his gloved hand deep under the blanket. And with a wobble of his chubby cheek's "No no no, definitely not!" well I rolled up. I put my hand up in a form of submission "I'm only joking Tuscan" I put the probe over my finger to show him it was harmless. I took it off again and showed him how it worked. I was still chuckling out loud. Finally I got Tuscan to remove his glove and I was able to put the probe on. "I've had less trouble putting that probe on children than I've had with you Tuscan!" some time after the probe had been put in place I was still outwardly chuckling away, Tuscan looked at me "Your mad!"

"No I'm not, in fact I'm in extremely good sprits today"

"No not that sort of mad. I mean mad mad, as in nutter!" I looked at Tuscan, I knew what he meant in the first place, now he knew that I knew what he meant and I was taking the Mickey. I chuckled a bit more. Tuscan finally cracked a smile

"You bloody NHS professionals. I thought you were all supposed to have an impeccable bedside manner!"

"I have Tuscan, you're smiling aren't you?"

"I don't know. I totalled my bike, I've damaged my leg and I wind up with a nutter to take me to hospital" still smiling and shaking his head he went on

"What do you consider a good day?"

"Believe me Tuscan a good day for me is an extremely bad day for you! You really don't want to know!"

"You're nuts" he muttered. We continued our banter for the remainder of the journey and I handed over at A+E. We shook hands and I wished him well – we parted on good terms. I checked up on Tuscan later on and found out he had been released from A+E. He'd got a bruised and grazed knee, ah bless him!

The following day when I got into work someone grabbed me "there's a bouquet of flowers in the crew room for you"

"Me! You sure?" I was directed through to the main crew room that was packed with front line staff. On a small bookcase was a huge bouquet of flowers, it must have cost a few quid. As the general sarcasm, taunts and humorous remarks were being directed at me I grabbed the card that read, *to Chris the Paramedic. Keep up the bedside manner!*

Love Tuscan!!!.

Touchet to Tuscan. It took me months to live it down on station.

Chapter 9

The scars of Tuscan were slowly healing and I was becoming more confident with my skills. This particular sunny morning I was due to start at 8am, and amazingly enough I arrived at 7:45. My crewmate who I had been working with for three years was also in. Neither of us were morning people but we'd got our routine. Get the vehicle sorted, hit the toaster and down a brew before we got stuck into anything too taxing. We had a good understanding as a working crew and were good mates outside of work.

Before we'd had time to start our usual routine the encoder went off,

"Red call, for 46-year-old female. ?Kilo 1 (uncertified death) *GP on scene"*

With a GP on scene at a 46 year old sudden death and with no certification of death, meant the GP was going to be working on the patient. In short doing CPR. There was no hesitation from us. We threw our kit in the back of the motor and away we went. Malc drove like Stirling "Bloody" Moss on steroids! Rush hour traffic and a journey of about seven miles. It was a busy spring morning and we had to make our way to a village North of the city. Malc nailed it in eight mins and he kept all the corners of the vehicle in tact. An incredible drive given the time of day.

We arrived at a very well presented semi, grabbed our de-fib and resus bag and went to the front door which opened as we approached. We were directed upstairs by two lads in there twenties who we assumed were the patients' sons. Quite obviously shaken with the situation they found themselves in. I could smell fresh paint as we climbed the stairs. At the top we turned right into lovely warm master bedroom with thick pile carpet on the floor. On the bed was the 46-year-old lifeless patient with the GP getting on with CPR. As we broke our kit out the GP gave us the history:-

The patient woke at about 7am with central chest pain and breathless. She called the GP who arrived some 40 mins later. The GP noticed she was quite pale and sweaty and considered she was having some form of cardiac episode. The GP had given the patient 300mg of Aspirin (standard practice). The GP was just thinking of the next line of action when the patient sat up in bed and said I don't feel very well, clutched her chest and collapsed. Her resp's and pulse were absent when the GP took them. The GP then got one of her sons to call us. Since the GP had called there had been no output (no pulse).

The problem with doing CPR on a bed is that the bed bounces each time you try to compress the chest, and so it reduces the effectiveness of the CPR. However a bit of CPR is better than none at all. And to be fair to the GP a dead body is not easy to move.

Malc and myself moved the patient onto the floor. We'd got our ventilating kit organised and the oxygen attached. I cracked on with ventilating and Malc carried out the compressions. After a minute or so of some half tidy CPR I carried out one man CPR whilst Malc stripped the top half of the patients body and got her wired up to the De-Fib. After the leads had been put in place we stopped CPR and had a look at the rhythm on the screen.

"VF on the screen" I said to Malc. VF (ventricular fibrillation) is where the heart is fibrillating (a bit like a muscle spasm). This is due to lots of areas of the cardiac muscle producing their own electrical impulses and this creates lots of little contractions of the heart muscle instead of one big one. As a result the heart muscle never contracts properly and therefore no blood, or at least very little blood circulates around the body. Net result from that if untreated? Death!!! The idea of de-fibrillating (shocking) someone is to give the heart a dose of electricity which forces the heart muscle to contract. Hopefully the shock will knock out the unwanted impulses and the natural impulse will continue and not be impeded by lots of nascence impulses. This will hopefully restore the normal electrical activity of the heart. Giving the heart a big ole slap really!! This is very much a salvageable rhythm.

"Charging to 200 Joules" I said to Malc. The de-fib started to charge with it's familiar whirring noise lasting about 15 seconds with a long bleep at the end of the charging cycle.

"De-fib charged, checking patient, (to make sure she was still unconscious) checking screen, (to make sure the rhythm hadn't changed) stand clear, shocking now"

BOSH! As I hit the shock button the patient juddered with the electrical current that was delivered to her body.

"Check pulse" we checked for pulses in her neck (carotid) and wrist (radial) for about 10 seconds with nothing found. We checked the screen she was still in VF

"Charging to 200 Joules" once again the machine started its whirring sound followed by the high pitched bleep.

"Checking patient, checking screen, stand clear, shocking now"
BOSH! For a second time with the patient juddering once again.
"Check pulse" 10 seconds past, still no pulse.
I checked the screen again the patient was still in VF.
"Charging to 360 Joules"
BOSH!

"Check pulse" 10 seconds past, no pulse. As we checked the screen we saw that she was now in Asystole. Asystole is where the heart has completely lost any form of electrical activity and is still. It shows up on the screen as a flat-line, just like you see in all those hospital dramas! This is not a shockable rhythm and the remit we are taught is to revert back to good ole CPR and treat with drugs.

Malc cracked on with one-man-CPR and I got my intubation and I/V access equipment together. We quickly organised ourselves so that when he finished his two inflations he would move out of the way to allow me to get in and intubate, giving us a patent airway but allowing him to maintain the compressions. This would give me about 45 seconds to intubate before the patient was due for another inflation.

"After the next inflations mate" I said

"Ok mate. 12, 13, 14, 15" As the compressions were done.

"1st inflation 2nd inflation, in you come Chris" Malc moved to the right side of the patient and I huddled down at the patients head end. I opened up my laryngoscope blade to activate the light in the tip of the blade. I put the blade into her open mouth which lit up her tongue. I swept her tongue to the left and could see a small puddle of white saliva that had gathered in the airway during CPR.

"Have you got the suction unit there mate?"

"Here you go" Malc handed me the hissing suction catheter and under the illuminated light of the laryngoscope I was able to clear the saliva away to reveal the epiglottis, a small flap of muscle that covers the airway, it stops food etc going down the wrong way. I manoeuvred the laryngoscope blade under her epiglottis and gently lifted it to reveal the white vocal cords marking the entrance to the airway. "Stop CPR for a minute mate" Malc stopped CPR so I could advance the tube between her vocal cords. I watched the tip of the tube disappear into the airway followed by the deflated cuff. I attached the ventilator bag and gave a ventilation. Once the cuff was inflated I gave a further inflation whilst listening to her chest with the stethoscope. There was good air entry and no escaping of air around the inflated tube.

"Confirm intubation mate" Malc continued with his compressions. I moved to the patients left side to see if I could gain I/V access. When Malc had completed his 15 compressions he moved to the patients head end and gave two inflations followed by a further 15 compressions. Malc had already put a tourniquet on and I could see a vein that looked as if it would be a viable cannulation site, below the very pale sweaty surface. I took a cannula and advanced it through the skin and into the vein. I got an instant flash back. As always I flushed the cannula to confirm it's placement. We now had I/V access.

"Ok mate lets have a look at the screen again" still in Asystole. I had already got the drugs pack open and the course of action now was to start our drug regimes. I gave 1MG of Adrenaline I/V and pushed it through with 5 Mil's of sterile water. We then carried on with another two minutes of CPR. We stopped and checked the screen again and both of us felt for pulses. "No pulse and no change on the screen!" Malc said. Another 1MG of adrenaline flushed through with sterile water and followed by two minutes of CPR. I was pondering the next few moves we would be taking as I was ventilating the patient when Malc said "Check pulse" I put my fingers across her carotid pulse area and Malc checked for a radial pulse.

"I got an output mate" Malc said, who by now had got a bit of a sweat on. "I've got one as well mate" and there was a steady bleep, bleep, bleep coming from the De-Fib. Malc had spotted the changes in her ECG rhythm on the De-Fib screen whilst I'd been in a little world of my own thinking too far ahead. The rhythm on the screen could have been mine, it was perfect. Malc and myself looked at each other in amazement and we had a little smile at each other. The GP who, after her initial shock of the patient arresting, had thinned out and let Malc and me get on with it. The GP now started chipping on about "come on lets get her moved then, lets go"

"Nah" was a very swift answer!

As I've said earlier, to move someone is quite a delicate operation. It's well known within the Ambulance service that if someone is critically ill, more often than not, as you go to move them they wind up arresting. We weren't about to let all our work go to waste. And with this potentially being our first successful resus we were not about to rush.

We reasoned with the GP that this was still a very unstable patient and we wanted to make her as stable as possible before we attempted to move her. After a bit of healthy debate the GP relented and allowed us to play it our way. We continued to ventilate for about 15 minutes. We had got some fluids up to assist her with her blood pressure and we had got our pulse oximeter on to ensure we were perfusing her adequately. Most of the time her reading was about 98%-99% which is slightly better than the oximetry you would find on a long term smoker. So we were more than happy. Malc was having some cooling down time and chatting to the GP when I noticed the patient was chomping on the airway tube. "Oi Malc what do you reckon about this?" Malc looked and confirmed what I was thinking. She was trying to make her own respiratory effort. This can sometimes happen with a successful resus. As they become more conscious the patient starts to chomp on any foreign airways that have been put into place. It's all to do with the gag reflex returning as brain activity increases through good cerebral perfusion. Whilst this is a very encouraging sign the down side is that if you had a tube down your throat the only thing you would want to do is chuck! Needless to say this would compromise the airway. The way around this is to extubate (take out the tube). It's not complicated. Basically as the patient breaths in all the airways open to their maximum, so the cuff on the tube is deflated and as the patient breaths in, the tube is pulled out with no damage to the airway. This I did and then used the ventilator bag to supplement the breaths she wasn't taking. This again is problematic. If the patient now vomits you have no way of securing the airway to stop any vomit going into the lungs. Also because you are forcing air into the lungs, an element of it goes into the stomach and this can also induce vomiting. However, because the patient is improving the airway may protect itself, fingers crossed. The vomiting aspect didn't worry me too much as I figured with it being early morning the chances are she hadn't just eaten a roast dinner followed by half a bottle of Cabernet Sauvignon! (red wine for short), and anything she would have eaten yesterday would have long been digested. We assisted ventilation for about 10mins and as each minute passed she slowly started to improve her own respiratory rate. It got to the stage where we no longer had to assist her breathing in any way at all. We put her onto 100% Oxygen and left her almost to her own devices for another 5 minutes or so.

"Ok mate I think it's time to make a move" Malc agreed. It becomes almost 2nd nature to talk to patients even when they're unconscious. So as normal I went into my usual spiel "Sue, were going to move you do you understand me"? And to my amazement she nodded her head. Malc and I looked at each other stunned. I carried on "first of all I need to sit you up" Sue nodded again. I carefully sat her forward so I was behind her and rested her against my crouched leg. "Well done Sue. Now I need you to put your arms across your chest if you can" Sue acknowledged again and moved her arms as I had asked her to do. I'd been involved in some successful resus's before but I'd never had a response like this. To say I was blown away by it all is an understatement. By now Sue was on the carry chair and ready to move down the stairs. We did a final assessment and off to the Ambulance. Once we got Sue onto the stretcher we re-assessed again. All of Sue's observations were in order and it was as if she had just fainted but the ECG history told a completely different story. Whilst we weren't having deep and meaningful conversations about the financial depression of some, third world country all the signs were very encouraging.

We pre-alerted the local A+E and quite frankly I don't think they believed us. We arrived about 15mins later to the usual vast reception of the resus team, handed Sue over complete with ECG history, and a letter that the GP had put together. I think at that point they finally started to believe what we were saying. Whilst they went about doing all their tests Malc and I thinned out and went for a brew and a smoke. It's such a weird feeling after a job like that, it's not that you've potentially saved a life, or that the family are grateful, it's just knowing that you got it right in one of the most stressful situations you can be asked to encounter during your working day. The adrenaline rush turns to almost excitement and I can only liken it to stepping off of the biggest, baddest rollercoaster you've ever encountered. Your stomach's rolling, your hands are quivering and your heads buzzing but actually you're calming down and just want to go and do it all again, madness, pure madness! But bloody good fun.

After a swift brew and a 15 minute break we wandered back into the resus room to chat with the nurses about Sue. Once again Sue amazed us. As we chatted to one of the nurses, Sue put her hand on my shoulder still with her eyes closed "are you Chris or Malcolm?"

"I'm Chris"

"Thanks Chris and thank Malcolm when you see him"

"I'm here as well Sue"

"Thanks Malcolm" I can't recall what we replied as I was a bit numbed by the whole experience. We went outside for another swift brew trying to take in this crazy, crazy world in which we work. Sue was released from Hospital some 10 days later. She had some cardiac muscle damage which was to be expected but has basically made a full recovery.

Chapter 10

Time had moved on and the Reliable V6 Transit Ambulances had been retired. They had started to be replaced with an American imported ambulance that had a whacking great 6.6 litre engine. Nought to sixty mph in about as many seconds and on a good day would muster a devastating 75mph. To drive they were a complete handful, they were designed for Downtown Sunshine Boulevard with soft suspension and an automatic gearbox. They also had the turning circle of an ocean going oil tanker. Compared to the tranny's (ford transits) they were huge. They had a box on the back that wasn't too much smaller than my garage. To work in the back was a joy with all the room you could ask for, providing you were stationary. As soon as any speed was reached they would bounce around like being in a bouncy castle and being seated was the only real option. They had an impressive light show with blues all the way around and it was the first vehicle we'd had with the automated flashing high-beam head lights (wig-wag). It was also fitted with a PA system. Of course this didn't get abused much! There was a bit of gossip going around that the persons responsible for ordering the vehicles had been away to America for a couple of holidays whilst all the negotiation and purchasing was going on. It was also rumoured that the supplying company had paid for these holidays. Who knows, I'm just a Paramedic! The staff using the vehicles were quite concerned with the stability of them. There was the obvious bouncy bouncy of the vehicles and we had heard through the grapevine that one had overturned. Another had gone out of control for no apparent reason at about 60mph. The crew was a training crew that had an instructor with them, so any horseplay was ruled out.

Malc and me got a call to an RTA out in the 'sticks'. It was a lovely sunny day, we had the air con on and windows down (I know your not supposed to) and off we trundled with me driving. The familiar bounce bounce bounce started and I adopted the usual driving technique. This wasn't a question of pointing the vehicle in the direction you wished to travel, it was more of a question of working out which way the vehicle was facing between bounces and correcting it to the direction you wish to travel. We were doing about 65mph on a main road in a rural area. This was as quick as you wanted to be going to be honest. We needed to turn left onto a B road to head out into the country. As we approached the junction, we could see the road we wanted to turn into, it was at about 45 degrees to the left of us. On a wide grassy verge on the inside of the bend was a 1940's land rover parked up with a couple of people sat in it. As we started to turn into the junction the back end broke away "OOPS" I steered into the skid in a futile attempt to try to regain control. As we skidded onto the opposite side of the road the offside wheels gripped onto the tarmac and lifted the nearside wheels off the ground. We seemed to be sat at an angle of 45 degrees for a lifetime. Directly in front of us now was a telegraph pole, a hedge and a field. As we wobbled across the road on two wheels I was unable to do anything other than brake. We eventually connected with the opposite curb and this was all the vehicle needed to take it the rest of the way onto it's offside. As the vehicle landed on its side there was a big bang and a judder. At this point I was hit in the side of the head by a Gucci new12 lead ECG that Malc and me had on trial (it weighted about 7kg) So the next 20secs or so I was happily oblivious to.

Apparently we skidded on our side along the grass verge missing the telegraph pole by the width of an atom and coming to rest with the front end about 2 feet from the hedge.

"Chris, you Ok?" no reply.

"Chris you Ok?" no reply.

"Chris you Ok?"

"Yeah, I'm fine mate, how you doing?"

"Bloody hell mate I thought you were dead" Feeling a bit groggy but gathering my senses I weighed up the situation. The radio mike had fallen off of its holder and was bouncing around in front of my face. For some reason I found this quite amusing and started to laugh. I realised the first thing I should do is contact control and give them a Sit-Rep. It was as if the mike bouncing around in front of me was being dangled by a superior force to remind me. At this point someone arrived at the front of the vehicle, it was one of the guys out of the land rover parked on the corner. As he peered in through the windscreen I tried to suppress my laughter and gave him the thumbs up and keyed up the mike

"Control, Charlie one two you receiving over?"

"Charlie one two go ahead"

"Charlie one two we're unable to continue. Vehicle on its side, both crew members unhurt, nothing else involved over."

"Sorry Charlie one two, did you say you were on your side!?"

"Roger to that, both crew members unhurt and nothing else involved. You will however need to mobilise another vehicle to the initial RTA over"

"Roger Charlie one two will do and I'll mobilise the police and an officer to you over"

"Charlie one two roger to that"

Formalities out of the way and it was time to get out. Malc had managed to open the passenger door and climb out so I followed suit. As I popped my head and shoulders out someone took a photograph of me, just what I needed.

"That does not go to the press" I remarked as I jumped down.

"No that's OK. This is going into the photograph album for the day"

"For the day?"

"We have two coachloads coming up to the airfield where they used to be stationed during the war. As part of the VE day celebrations we're putting a photograph album together of the day. This'll give us something to chuckle about" I figured it could have been worse.

Malc and me beavered around taking all the gases out of the vehicle just in case there was a fire. The inside of the vehicle was wrecked, it looked like a bomb had hit it. This all reinforced the safety issues that had been highlighted. We got ourselves sorted out and disappeared into the field for a nerve settling smoke. The crew who had been mobilised to the initial RTA arrived at our location and stopped to see if we were ok. They also informed us that the officer who had been mobilised to us was 'exocet'. He was a complete git. He had gained the nickname 'exocete' due to his excellent management skills of handling people. In short if he had a problem with you he wouldn't find out all the facts by conversation. He would arrive in your space and just explode and there was nothing you could do to stop it from happening. Hence 'exocet'! He had also played a part in the purchasing of the vehicles and I knew he wasn't going to be my best buddy for the next few hours.

The crew continued to the RTA and as sure as eggs are eggs two coach loads of tourists arrived at their RV point with the land rover. They all disembarked and had a great laugh at our expense whilst clicking away with their cameras. A further five minutes past and the police arrived. He came over and asked what had happened. So I gave him a blow-by-blow account of what went on filling in the bits that Malc had told me! "Oh yes its quite obvious what's happened" said the cop "If you look, this road has recently been resurfaced. If you look at the middle of the junction its about 1" deep with stones. You can see where your tyres came over the stone and started to skid. Once you've got onto the compressed road your tyres have gripped and flipped you over. Isn't there a problem with these vehicles anyway?"

"Umm, allegedly" Just as I was finishing off 'exocet' arrived, "ooeck here we go" I said to the cop "This bloke's been involved with the purchasing of the vehicles. Figure his jobs on the line. He's not going to be happy"

The traffic cop looked at 'exocet' then looked back at me "don't worry its fine" He walked off to meet 'exorcete' away from us. But 'exocet' had made his way to the two witnesses who had seen it happen. There was a lot of pointing and head nodding going on between 'exocet' and the two witnesses. The cop managed to gain 'exocet's' attention. There was more head nodding and pointing from the cop as he was explaining what he thought had gone on. But 'exocet' was looking in my direction and not really paying any attention. As expected, 'exocet' had heard enough and headed towards us "Impact 5 secs" I said to Malc. The problem I had was that I'd been rallying for about three years. 'Exocet' knew this as we'd spoken about it in the past, or at least he'd said to me "if I find you rallying my ambulances I'll have ya sacked" This information he had was not going to make my life any easier. However the traffic cop had already given me his thoughts and I felt reasonably safe.

"What the bloody hell have you been doing?" he barked.

"Checking out to see if it was less bouncy on its side" Perhaps wasn't the best answer I've ever given but what the hell!

"I bet you were practising your rallying"

"You can think what you want but let me assure you, your wrong"

"We'll see about that"

"Fine by me" 'exocet' looked at the cop and hollered "I want the crash investigation team to find out what's gone on"

"I'm not sure that'll be necessary"

"I want it done properly. With an investigation and documentation, do you understand?"

"Well I'll have to speak to my skipper about that"

"Give me his name I'll phone him" The cop gave the name of his skipper and 'exocet' left the scene forgetting one vital thing, us! The idea of him coming out was to make sure the crew are ok, wait for the recovery vehicle and then return us to the station! Not that we were to bothered. I think if we had been in each others company for too long he would have probably wound up with a right hook. The cop looked at us in amazement "is he always like that?"

"Yup" he shook his head in disbelief.

The novelty of an ambulance being up-ended had now worn off and everyone had left the scene leaving Malc and me on our own. We relaxed for a while in the afternoon sun having a chuckle at 'exocet's' expense and waited for the recovery vehicle to arrive. When it arrived an hour or so later we managed to convince the driver to take us back to base although this wasn't his job. We found using bribes of cups of tea and the fact that the vehicle couldn't have been de-kitted on the side of the road due to it's unsafe state, seemed to work. He knew we were having him over but agreed all the same. If Malc and me really wanted to we could have climbed back into the ambulance called up control and got someone else to pick us up. But quite frankly if 'exocet' had been sent out again there would have been bloodshed!

In the following months the crash investigation team did their work and the internal investigation unfolded. Malc and me were called into the office by numerous officers on many occasions, usually with no warning and never offered any form of representative. I think in a grown-up work place it would have been called a kangaroo court, but it's the sort of thing you get used to in the Ambulance Service. However we stuck to our guns and told it how it was. Unfortunately for Malc he was the passenger involved in another roll over in one of the Yank tank's about a month after ours. Understandably he totally refused to ride in them after that. Couldn't blame him really, but what that meant was each time we came to work we had to go out in the station spare which was usually the biggest heap on station, but even that felt more secure than an American Wobbly Bus! The crash investigation team came up with the same conclusion as the traffic cop did at the scene. It was also concluded that the vehicles were unsafe at speed. Something to do with them being top heavy and a 60mph restriction was slapped on all the American Wobbly Buses. How proud were we. The cutting edge of pre-hospital emergency care toddling down the motorway at 60mph!

Shortly after the dust had settled from our little roll, two of the officers who were involved in the purchasing took early retirement. Yep you've guessed it, 'exocete' has gone and what a loss he'll be to the service!! Unfortunately due to budgets and the lack of funds the wobbly Buses had to remain. The robust and reliable Tranny's had been decommissioned, stripped out and sold off. To my knowledge we have one remaining Wobbly Bus as a legacy and a reminder of what not to buy. As for the rest? The last I heard a majority of them were only fit for selling Kebab's and Bacon butties at car boot sales!

Chapter 11

Malc had seen an advert in one of the Ambulance Service Magazines for a Paramedic to work out in Saudi. He'd answered the add and gone for the interviews. He'd been successful and had moved out to Saudi. Now he had left I was working with various crewmates. One particular morning I was working with a guy from another station. A call came in at about 7:15am to one of the outer villages that we cover. Off we went with me at the wheel on yet another damp grey morning. We got onto a straight piece of road in a built-up area about half a mile from the station when we caught up with a truck. I moved over to the crown of the road to see if the road ahead was clear to make an overtake. There was a car coming towards us at about 100 meters away. No chance for an overtake but plenty of time to pull back in, which I did. I was now unable to see the car coming towards us due to the height of the truck so waited until it had passed to take another look.

As I settled back onto my side of the road I heard the noise of skidding tyres on a wet surface. As I looked passed the lorry the car that was coming towards us had locked up and was skidding. It hit a bus shelter on its side of the road and ricocheted back towards us heading for the front end of the Ambulance. I swerved to the left to avoid a collision working my hands quickly like a demented Hamster on its wheel. The car just missed our front end. That was close I thought, then I heard a big bang. I had to swerve back to the right to avoid mounting the kerb and hitting a lamppost. The ambulance went up onto the two nearside wheels and we went across the road (here we go again I thought). I managed to get the left hand lock on and bring the vehicle down onto four wheels again. We skidded to a halt in the entrance to a secondary school. I looked at my mate "you all right?"

"A bit shaken, bloody well driven, I thought we were a gonna"

"So did I! More luck than judgement I reckon. Can you let control know" I got out of the vehicle to go to the car driver. As I walked back I looked at the damage to the ambulance. The rear offside corner had been knocked completely out and I could peer into the back of the Ambulance through the hole. Also the rear wheel had been hit and the rear axle had been somewhat rearranged and was sitting a few degrees out. As I walked towards the car there were pieces of fibreglass all over the road and a piece of 2X2 box section metal lying on the road. The Ambulance had been totalled. As I walked towards the car I could hear screaming from it. As I approached the driver's door I could see a young female with her head in her hands screaming for England. I opened the door and shouted "HELLO" She ignored me. "HELLO" this time I grabbed her hands and pulled them away from her face.

"Can you hear what I'm saying to you?"

"YES" came the reply in a broken, loud voice.

"Are you ok or have you been hurt?"

"NO, I'M OK" she was absolutely hysterical.

"Come on lets have you out of the car" her hysteria became worse.

"What's wrong?"

"WHO'S DEAD WHO'S HURT?"

"No ones dead, no one's hurt. Come on lets have you out of the car"

"ARE YOU SURE NO ONES HURT? WHAT ABOUT THE AMBULANCE DRIVER? "

"He's all right, that was me. Now STOP SHOUTING AT ME. Lets have you out, you're in the middle of the road" she looked at me with her once well made-up face all running down her cheeks.

"You ok then?"

"Yes we're both fine, now out of your car " I grabbed her arm and started to usher her out.

"Wait a minute I need my mobile" she rummaged around in the back of her car and retrieved her handbag "I must call my boyfriend"

"That's fine by me but get onto the pavement first please" I walked her over to the pavement "keep away from your car until the police arrive and start traffic control" she nodded in agreement whilst concentrating on what number she dialled. The last thing I needed was for her to get wiped out whilst fetching her favourite rabbits foot hanging from the rear-view mirror! I hooked up with my crewmate, he'd informed control and they in turn would notify the police. At this point I heard some sirens coming up the road. I figured another vehicle was going out on another job. As they got to our incident they pulled over. It was a good friend of mine, hippie-Jim. His name came about by way of his laid back nature, long hair, love of Irish music and always turned out looking like he'd fell out of the bottom of the ironing basket. "Allo, Chris you all right?"

"Yup, cocker-hoot" he gave me the once up and down and saw there were no injuries, "You been banger racing again ain't ya" Jim remarked with a big ole smile.

"Something like that. What you doing here anyway?"

"We were told you'd been involved in a head on ole mate. Thought you may need a bit of assistance with ya broken bones old boy"

"Cheeky bugger. You're the one who'll need assistance with busted bones you carry on like that" I chuckled back.

"Seriously though mate you ok? Anything you need?

"Yup, a smoke"

"Come on then lets go round the back of the hedge" With that we both heard sirens coming up the road. We paused for a minute and eventually we could see an ambulance officer's car coming up the road followed by the police.

"Hang-fire Jim lets see who that is first. I've had some bad experiences with officers tipping out to ambulance RTA's!" As the car pulled in I could make out the figure of another good friend of mine. He had moved into training and was heading very quickly to become the head of training. We had also been crewmates for nearly a year, so knew each other really well. It was his fault that I had gained the nickname of 'Slapdash'. This was due to me breaking a lot of what I touched. And if someone is in the road with a fractured leg, I'm the most likely person to clip his wounded limb with my foot as I stepped over him. As the officer got to Jim and me he held out his hand to shake mine "Morning Slaps I know we wanted rid of this old tub but this is a bit extreme isn't it?

"Well someone had to do it!

"Everything in order?"

"I reckon mate, cops sorting the other driver out"

"Have they spoke with you yet?

"No, they just pulled up behind you didn't they!

"Oh yes of course. Never could do early mornings. Jim keeping you warm then"

"Well kind of. We were just off behind the hedge to have a smoke"

"Oh come on then slaps I'll join ya" We all made our way behind the hedge to keep out of the public gaze. As we stood smoking and chewing the fat. Jim came up with the fact that we were now behind the cycle sheds at a secondary school and how not much had changed since our school days. Sad but true.

The police took their usual statements and I waited for recovery for an hour or so. When he finally arrived this head poked out of the drivers window "You'll be putting the kettle on then, again! It was the same guy who had recovered me before. "Yes I'll be making the brews, again!" No police crash investigation team this time. However the service have a duty to follow up such incidents so there was still a low key investigation ongoing. But I figured that plain old bad luck would be the outcome and slapdash wrecks another motor!

A couple of weeks after the RTA the service started to advertise for RRV Drivers (Rapid Response Vehicle). The idea of having RRV's was due to new government legislation now requiring that we arrive on scene at any category 'A' call within eight minutes. Category 'A' being things like Chest pain, cardiac arrest and essentially anything that's considered life-threatening. The problem is that the ambulances can't cover the ground that quickly, no matter how good a driver you are. It's a big area that we cover and the Ambulance station is on the south/west side of the city. So something had to be put in place and the RRV cars seemed to be the obvious answer. This was a totally new concept for East Anglia and those who would be offered the posts had to be prepared to work on their own, thrash out rotas for the station RRV team and be responsible for the general running and up-keep of the cars. The position of an RRV Paramedic seemed like it would be a good crack mixed in with the pressure of being on your own. I tend to up the anti when under pressure, so thought it would also go some way to keep me from getting bored and thus out of trouble! All the applicants had to have at least two years post-qualification as a Paramedic, submit a CV and a case study of an incident they had attended. Those who got short-listed would then have a final interview.

The investigation from my last prang was still ongoing and I thought this would seriously hamper any submission of mine, but who dares wins and all that. So my application went in. A few days after the closing date I received a letter explaining that I had been short-listed for the RRV team and I would be informed of an interview date with in the next 14 days. A few days later I was buzzing around station in between jobs and was 'invited' into the office by my Station Officer. In the office was sat my County Commander. The County Commander, as the name suggests, is the person who runs the county vehicles and personnel. Basically what he say's goes. He was a guy called Glynn and he was known to be fair but quite hard with it at times. This was a bit of an unexpected meeting and I wasn't too sure what it was all about. It's not every day that you are called into the office by your bosses boss. I figured he wasn't about to ask me how my last holiday went or wish me happy birthday. As I walked into the office Glynn beckoned me to take a seat. My gut feeling was that this was not going to be a pleasant meeting. "Now then Chris I need to speak to you about this RTA you had some time ago"

"OK"

"A witness who you overtook just prior to the RTA said that you were going probably about 60mph, would that be so?"

"Yes it would be. It's a straight piece of road you can see plenty in front of you so why not?"

"Well it is a 30mph limit and a built-up area"

"That's true enough but quite frankly I can't see what the problem is. At that time of the morning there's little movement of other traffic and no pedestrians around so why not?"

"The problem is Chris that you've also got an application in for the RRV post. What sort of speed would you be doing in a car given the same conditions?" Oh shit was my thought process. I think I've just bombed out of any chance of getting an RRV post. Oh well it was to be expected.

"Well Glynn, probably about 60mph actually. Given the conditions and the time of day I think that 60mph is on the upper limits of being acceptable whether you are in a car or an Ambulance"

"What about if you had been in the car though, how do you think you would of come out of the RTA? Walking? Injured? Killed?"

"Well I probably would not of been involved in the RTA in the first place if I had been in a car"

"Why's that then?"

"Well we were going out to one of the outer villages so I wouldn't have been on that piece of road, I would have been on the main road. There's no point an ambulance going on the main road to that village as you have to cover more miles and it would actually take longer. But in an RRV using the main road would allow for greater speed and so would actually reduce my call to scene time. Isn't that what being on the RRV is all about?"

"OK but we can't afford to be repairing damaged RRV's all the time as this means they're off the road and not doing what they should be doing. So how would we stop someone having an accident in an RRV?"

"Not put them in it in the first place!" This answer probably wasn't going to do my RRV application any favours but it was an honest opinion and the most logical I could think of.

"So you don't think you should be offered a post on the RRV due to the accident you had" umm, tricky I thought to myself, could this be my interview for the RRV? I think Glynn knew my next answer and now had me by the short and curly's!

"No I don't think that at all"

"So, for argument sake, if you were offered a post on the RRV how could we make sure you don't have an accident?" I was unable to answer and felt myself fidget around in the chair. Squirming I think it's called! Glynn continued,

"OK, how about if I said we'll offer you a place on the RRV" my heart missed a beat "BUT, if you prang it you get the sack!"

"No way, absolutely not"

"Why not"

"Firstly, any accident may not be my fault, and secondly, I think there'll be quite enough going through my head without the worry of being sacked hanging over me. Besides, if the threat of being sacked is there surely the first thing I'll do is to slow down. What's the point of having a rapid response car if it doesn't rapidly respond!" Glynn thought for a minute while eyeballing me.

"OK, fair point. What about if we were to say 'should' you be offered a position on the RRV and wind up bending it that you get thrown off the team?"

"I think that would be totally fair actually"

"Good" there was a pregnant pause for a minute whilst Glynn looked at the paperwork in front of him. My heart started to accelerate a little bit waiting for the next curve ball to be delivered in my direction. Finally Glynn looked up "enjoy your time on the RRV but remember, if you bend it you're off!" It took me a moment or two to work out what Glynn had said and I still wasn't sure that what I heard, was what I was meant to of heard?

"Sorry, are you telling me that was my RRV job interview?"

"Yes"

"But what about that witness who said about the problem with my speed?"

"He never said there was a problem with your speed. He just said you were going about 60mph. It wasn't a criticism. You thought it was a criticism, so maybe you thought it was a bit quick and maybe that's something for you to think about for the future" There was a short pause as Glynn's eyes burnt their way into my head and the words he said were well and truly planted in my brain.

"Anyway, that's also the conclusion of the investigation into your RTA. There's nothing to be answered. Witness statements all check out with yours so its finished with. Nice to see you again Chris. I have to make a hasty retreat elsewhere, see ya again, bye" Glynn left the room and I'm sitting there thinking has this really just happened. It's the weirdest interview I'd ever had but Glynn had well and truly made his point. The git had been toying with me all along. Thankfully I stuck to my guns and argued my points.

Having just about scraped through the interview, and had provisionally been accepted onto the RRV team, there were a couple of weeks of training to be done and rotas to sort.

Chapter 12

All personnel who had been offered the provisional places on the RRV (rapid response vehicle) had been given the start date for the training and had assembled in a conference centre in Suffolk. This was all a bit new to me as most of the time any training that is undergone is usually along the lines of taking your own food along and muddling around in a room somewhere trying to make it into a classroom. On this occasion it was all a bit Gucci, purpose built, food laid on and tea and coffee on tap. We could pretty-well come and go as we pleased. Buzzing around between vehicle familiarisation and working through the various admin tasks that had to be done. The conference room was on the second floor and made up part of a courtyard area that looked as if it was probably an inn during the late 1700's. Typical Suffolk construction, big beams, quaint windows and a cobbled courtyard area in the middle. Most of the other buildings were being used by small commercial firms apart from one which was a pub and this is where we were going to be fed and watered! This was a tad torturous as obviously there was no drinking of alcoholic beverages during dinner. We weren't in a pass/fail situation so the atmosphere throughout was quite relaxed.

There were three of us on each car and seven cars throughout East Anglia. Each car could work whatever roster they wished providing we didn't work after 2am, as this was considered unsafe, or work more than our 40hrs per person per week. Mark was one of the other guys on the car, so him and me worked around the roster whilst Stuart, the third person on our car, started to get the kit together. We came up with a roster where we worked for most of the time 0700 to 1500 and 1500 to 2300. The exception to this was Friday and Saturday where we worked 0700 to 1600 and 1600 to 0200. The roster had been agreed so we could now turn our attention to the Car and kit. Unfortunately our car and three of the others hadn't been delivered so we could only organise our kit. Stuart had been getting the kit together, and some of that still hadn't arrived from the supplier, this is quite standard for the Ambulance service! Instead of having our usual paramedic boxes we were issued with backpacks. This was another first for the service and in most people's eyes was the way forward. We had two backpacks per car. One that we turned into a first response bag that had everything in it we would require for basic life support. The second we kitted with on going treatment equipment such as drugs and fluids etc. It took several days to get the backpacks kitted to what we considered to be the most user-friendly. We would kit it as we thought to be right then knock out a couple of scenarios, then kit it again to hopefully improve on our first thoughts. This was also good training to hone our skills and have a more slick working practice, and get used to the idea that there isn't a crewmate to be helping out. As much experience as we all had, working on our own was definitely a challenge. Everything seemed to happen in double-quick time, and when the scenarios had finished there was kit all over the place as if someone had picked up the bag and tipped it upside down. Also, because it was now one person having the thought process of two it was mentally tiring. After a week of practising re-kitting and practising again, we felt we had got the best set-up, but the proof wouldn't be known until the first call was out of the way.

The following week was an introduction to the cars that had now been finished and delivered. We all had our own ideas as to how the kit should be stowed in the backs of the cars. And providing the team were happy with the way their car was kitted then that was good enough. We also had to learn about a new piece of technology, satellite navigation, (SATNAV) such a cool bit of kit, bang in the address and let the women tell you where to go, situation normal then! The beauty of this woman is that you can turn the volume down!! For the duration of the next five days we had a police driving instructor with us and he would take it in turns to ride out with each car. He gave us heaps of tips to get the maximum speed out of the car. He was teaching us a much more aggressive way of driving, where as the ambulance service had taught us a more defensive form of driving. This was right up my street I loved the extra speed and road holding available with the car. By the end of each session with him the brakes would be smoking and smelling after they had been given a hammering on the little country roads of Suffolk. When he wasn't with us we would tap an address into the SATNAV to, for example, High Street of a nearby village and then follow the directions. We also started to make use of distances given out by SAT-NAV to the next road junction. We soon learned that 100 meter warning to the next turn was also useful information to be used as a braking point prompt. Half way through the week we had to do some off-road driver training, obviously this was immense fun and I was pleasantly surprised what the Honda CRVs were capable of. One of the spin-offs with the RRV was that it had off-road capabilities and could go where the conventional ambulances couldn't. In the past what we did as a crew, if we were in the middle of a field, was to call a second vehicle and carry the patient on a spinal board or scoop stretcher until we got to hard standing. The RRV was also equipped with a cage in the back mainly to stop all the kit coming forward under heavy braking. The cage could be re-configured so we could slide a spinal board in, and were able to drive to the hard standing with the patient thus not requiring another crew. All in all it was a good couple of weeks, lots learned and for once treated like adults. To finish the fortnight off we had a couple of press releases to do, photos and interviews with the local papers to publicise the RRV regional team. Apart from that we were finished and ready to go live Monday morning. Ooeck, once again.

By now I'd been on the RRV for just under two months and it hadn't been as busy as I'd expected it to be. Part of this was simply because I was in the wrong place at the wrong time so no point being sent. The other part of this was due to the controllers' not being used to having the RRV as an extra resource. As a result of this the RRV team monitored the radio throughout the shift and self activated on calls, calling up Control and telling them that we were now mobile to an incident. This didn't always make for a smooth relationship with the controllers and the RRV team, but it seemed to be the most efficient way of using the RRV's.

One evening I was working on the late shift and had been returned for my   half-hour break. When I got back to the Ambulance station, all the crews were out working. Control had phoned in order to stand me down for my break so I cranked up the microwave for my usual chicken ding. Before the oven had time to finish the controller rang again, "hi ya Chris we have a red for you" bang goes dinner then. They sent me to a location about three minutes drive from the Station. Someone had called 999 due to a cut leg. It's a known fact within the service that we all have a tendency to pre-judge jobs before we arrive on scene. The main reason for this is that we try to be organised before we get to the location but the down side to this is, if we pre-judge a job and we consider it a waste of time, such as a cut finger, or, a non injury fall, we can be in the wrong frame of mind when we arrive. As far as I was concerned this fell into the category of 'OH it's a cut leg' and I was bloody hungry and thus the job carried a priority of zero! En-route I was updated by Control who repeated that they had no other vehicles available to back me up at this stage. I said to them not to worry about back up as I could probably deal with this on my own. I knew the location I was going to as being retirement flats, so I didn't have a feeling that there was going to be any physical trouble. Generally when the elderly cut themselves it's due to paper thin skin that requires no more than cleaning, dressing and referring them to their GP for follow on treatment.

As I arrived at the location I could see the flat about 10 meters the other side of a grassed area with a patio stone pathway leading to the front door. It was pretty much in darkness with a dim light defusing through the front door glazing. I grabbed my backpack and approached the front door. I knocked at the door and waited, no reply. A second, harder knock gave me the same result. I opened the letterbox to shout through and could just about make out a spattering of blood on the floor. As my eyes adjusted to the gloom it was quite apparent there was a lot of blood about in the hallway. I shouted through the letterbox "HELLO AMBULANCE SERVICE" and then placed my ear against the open letterbox. I could here a faint "come in" I turned the door handle and cracked the door open slightly "HELLO" Once again I could just hear a faint "come in" I opened the door about halfway so I could see the length of the hallway. The hallway floor was covered in light grey tiles with a thin dark rug running up the middle of it with the usual magnolia finish to the walls. At the far end of the hallway was a room to the right with a blood trail coming from it and looked as if it went into a room opposite. The trail then came down the hallway and off to my right into what I thought was the kitchen. The blood trail running from room to room and down the hallway was about 6 to12 inches wide with the imprint of footmarks throughout its length. The blood also went 3 to 4 inches up the wall as if someone had used the wall to hold themselves up and the injured leg had been closest to the wall. I shouted again "HELLO"

"In here" came a faint voice to my right and where another dim light was coming from. I took a careful half step forward and looked to my right. With the dim light I could make out a gallery type kitchen about 6ft in length with units either side. There was a pool of blood covering most of the kitchen floor this continued up some of the units and into the sink. I could see a couple of blood sodden wads of tissues in the sink and another on the floor where someone had obviously tried to sort out whatever wounds they had received. About halfway down the kitchen was a male in his 70's with a bald head wearing underwear only. He was lying on the floor with his shoulders propped up by a unit. He looked extremely pale and sweaty, taking deep breaths with blood still flowing freely out of his left leg. As I slowly approached him I said,

"Hello fella, what you been up to then?"

"I've caught my leg on the bath side" He said in a weak voice.

"How long ago did this happen?"

"About thirty minutes" his voice weakened and he fell unconscious. His head fell forward, partially occluding his airway that now produced a snoring noise and he started to list to the left. I put my knee against his left should to stop him falling any further and managed to get my hands either side of his head with my palms over his ears and my fingers under his jaw. I lifted his chin up and his jaw forward to try to regain some form of open airway for him. At the same time I slowly moved my knee away from his shoulder so he fell towards me with a controlled movement so that I could lower his shoulders and head to the ground. I took hold of his wrist to feel a pulse. He was clammy to touch and he had no pulse in his wrist. I felt for a pulse in his neck and could feel a weak, thready and fast pulse and this also confirmed he was still breathing. I opened up my bag and took out the oxygen.

"Come on fella lets get ya on the road to recovery" I muttered. I connected the oxygen cylinder to the mask and placed it over his nose and mouth. I turned my attention to his leg injury. He still had blood coming from the injury that was about an inch long. He had yellow fatty tissue around the injury which indicated the injury was quite deep. I grabbed a dressing from the bag and placed it over the wound putting quite a lot of pressure on the bandage as I tied it off. Now with the oxygen in place, the bleeding arrested and the wound dressed I wanted to raise his legs to assist with getting the oxygen to his brain. The only thing to hand was a kitchen bin. I flipped it onto its side allowing the rubbish to start tipping out and went to place it under his ankles. At this point I could feel his legs start to shake as I looked him up and down he went into a full-blown convulsion. His right arm was rattling the base of the unit that he was originally propped up against and his head was gently but rapidly bouncing off of the floor. I made a hasty move back towards his head to replace the mask that was now on his forehead. After doing so I got my hands under his shoulders and rotated him away from the cupboards. This was made easier by the blood over the floor acting almost as a lubricant between him and the lino. I clamped my hands either side of his head again and my fingers under his jaw to lift his chin, whilst with my thumbs I held the O2 mask in place. By now I was on all 4's with knees, elbows and forearms being dunked in the blood covered floor. *Its not uncommon with patients that have lost a lot of blood to go into a fit caused by Hypoxia (Lack of adequate tissue perfusion, I.e. not enough oxygen going around the body) in this patient's case he has lost a lot of blood (hypovolemic shock, i.e. the lack of volume of blood within the circulatory system) which had reduced his blood pressure. If there isn't enough blood pressure the oxygen is unable to travel from the circulating blood into the muscles, tissue and ultimately the brain. With the brain being starved of oxygen it has caused him to fit.* Ultimately I needed to get some fluids into him but this was out of the question for the time being. I'd already taken a risk and left his airway unsecured (a cardinal sin) so I could stop the haemorrhage and was now paying the price with him. It's a judgement call you have to make when your working on your own, bend the SOP's (standard operating procedures) a bit. All I could do for the time being was play the waiting game get loads of oxygen into him and try to reverse the hypoxic fit he was having. After what seemed like an eternity, but realistically was only a minute or so, his fit subsided and he became motionless once again. I felt for a pulse in his wrist and it was still absent. I took my I/V kit out of the bag and tightened the tourniquet around his bicep. I went back to his airway to make sure it was still open whilst the veins in the lower part of his arm swelled as they slowly filled with blood. It was hard to see exactly what was going on with his veins in the dim light so I used my pen torch to keep a check. Once they had filled to some form of workable size I moved away from his airway and took hold of his arm. With the pen torch in my mouth as extra light I studied the veins to select a vein that I considered to be my best chance of getting an I/V line in. Most of the veins were still quite thready except for one on the inside joint of the elbow (right median cubital or anti cubital fossa, depending what books you read) I took out a 14 gauge cannula and very carefully lined up and advanced the needle, direct hit. I gave myself an inward sigh of relief. I anchored the cannula in place and connected up a giving set (a tube just over a meter long, that connects the bag of fluid to the cannula) and the bag of I/V fluid. Once everything was connected I opened the valve of the giving set and let the fluid run through as quick as it could (stat, as the Americans say on all there ER programmes). I hooked the bag onto a cupboard handle to give it the height it needed and moved back to his airway. He was still clammy but not quite as grey as he had been. The oxygen had started to assist him greatly. I got the pulse oximeter out, switched it on and placed it on his finger. After the machine had settled down it started to give me an oxygen saturation reading that was quite healthy considering all that had gone on before. His pulse rate was still fast but that was to be expected. Once again I was playing the waiting game while the fluid bolstered up his BP (Blood Pressure) and the oxygen worked at refreshing his brain.

Earlier in the book I spoke about getting the balance between blood loss and fluid replacement correct and how over-or under-infusion is detrimental to the casualties health. In this present situation it's going to be unlikely that I'm going to over-infuse the patient. The blood that was around the flat was greater than the volume I had in the I/V bag. Even if I did over infuse him his injury is totally different to the maternity. He has got an external bleed that can be easily controlled in the pre-hospital environment, unlike an internal bleed, which is still easy to diagnose, but very difficult to manage.

Whilst playing the waiting game I was mulling over the options in my mind about the next course of treatment if he didn't regain consciousness. And thoughts of moving him out to the Ambulance once the crew arrived! Arh, of course. The crew aren't going to arrive until I contact Control. Because I've told them I probably wouldn't need a crew. I can be sooo clever sometimes! And the mobile phone? In the car. As I've previously stated communications are everything when you're on your own. Hey-Ho, I'll learn one day I'm sure!

The first unit of fluid had gone through and I'd left his airway unprotected again in favour of putting a second unit up. As I was in the process of this I saw flicker from his eyes. "Hello fella how ya feeling?" I got no reply. Instead he stared straight up at the ceiling eyes wide open. I opened the valve wide open again, hooked the bag onto the handle and went back to his airway and controlled his head and jaw again. I thought he was going to fit again. After I had control of his head I repeated the question "Hello fella how ya feeling?" he blinked and mumbled something that I couldn't understand but it was a step forward. After 30seconds or so I repeated the question "Hello fella, how ya feeling?"

"Not to bad I'm a bit cold" a bit bloody cold! I was sweating like I'd been in a sauna! "OK mate I'll get that sorted out for you shortly. What do I call you by the way?"

"Jim"

"OK Jim, apart from being cold how do you feel?"

"A little bit dizzy. Where am I?"

"You are on your kitchen floor at the moment, you took a bit of a funny turn"

"I seem to remember fainting"

"Yes Jim, you have had a bit of a faint"

"Why's that happened then?"

"Well you've cut your leg Jim. It probably all stems from that"

"I remember catching my leg on the bath and trying to stop the bleeding, is that what's caused me to faint then? Its never happened before"

"The thing is Jim you've lost a lot of blood from your leg and its put your blood pressure in your boots mate"

"Oh I see. How bad is my leg then?"

"Its not too bad but I assume you caught a varicose vein and they tend to bleed quite a lot, but its stopped now. How you feeling at the moment?"

"Not too bad actually"

"Do you still feel dizzy?"

"No just cold"

"Can you tell me what today is?"

"Wednesday"

"What about the month?"

"November"

"What about the date Jim, any ideas?"

"Umm about the 15th I think"

"To be honest Jim I'm not too sure myself" Jim had a little smile at my shortfall

"OK Jim, I'm going to go to the car and get a blanket for you. You're going to be OK for a couple of minutes?"

"Could I get onto a chair do you think?"

"Not just at the moment Jim, there are a few other things I need to do first, then we'll see about getting you off the floor" Jim was making excellent progress but standing up at the moment was not high on my agenda. I went out to the car and picked up the microphone. "*Control this is 616 are you receiving over?*"

"*616, I was just getting concerned about you, you've been on scene quite a long time. Is everything OK over?*"

"*It's a long story. Are there any crews available over?*"

"616 roger to that. I have one just cleared at Addenbrookes, they'll be with you shortly over"

"616 much appreciated" I opened the boot, picked up a blanket and made my way back to the flat. "Hi ya Jim how you doing?"

"Not too Bad lad" Jim was feeling better.

"Here's a blanket for you" I covered him over and continued with my assessment. His radial pulses were now back, his colour was now pink and he was no longer sweating. I took his BP, that had returned to almost normal, as had his pulse rate. Nice one I thought to myself.

"Now then Jim I've called an ambulance for you. You need to go up to the Hospital to get your leg checked out and repaired. Is that OK Jim?"

"Well if you think that's the best thing to do that's fine by me"

"All things considered Jim, I think it's for the best Mate"

"Ok then" I could hear the vehicle pulling up outside "I'm just popping outside again Jim, I'll be back soon" I went out to greet the crew and give them a hand over out of ear-shot of Jim. I didn't want to panic him too much as he was now well on the road to recovery and I didn't want any setbacks. As I approached the crew one of them looked at me and said "What on earth have you been up to Chris?" as I took a look at myself my boots were covered in blood. My trousers from the knees down were covered in blood, as was my jacket on the front where it had been undone and dragged on the floor. The forearms of my coat were sodden where I'd been supporting Jim's head while he fitted.

"Well guys this is how things unfolded" I took them through an account of how the job unfolded and what the state of play was now. We all made our way back into Jim's flat, got him off the floor and away to Hospital.

"Control this is 616 are you receiving over?"

"616 go ahead"

"Control, I'm clear on scene over"

"616 I have another job for you over"

"Err, No!" I explained my reason and was returned to base to clean up and have a well earned brew.

A few days later I checked up on Jim. He had been discharged from hospital but had gone to a Hospice. During his stay in Hospital they had gone through the usual examinations and found that he'd got skin cancer. Jim being the type of stoic person he was hadn't been to his GP. Unfortunately for Jim and after further assessment he was found to have cancer of the throat and was unlikely ever to return home.

Chapter 13

Our initial thoughts about the RRV were that it should go out in the 'sticks' so that we could use its speed to get across country to the far to reaching villages. The thoughts were sound but during the two months that I'd been on the RRV I'd become frustrated as there hadn't been the workload I'd expected. I felt this was mainly due to the RRV being deployed to the wrong locations. Despite conversations with my boss, my words seemed to fall on deaf ears. It wasn't that he didn't take any notice of what I was saying it was more down to him having to run the regional RRV team that was spread over the entire area of East Anglia, some 5000 square miles. It's a huge area with an overwhelming workload of admin for him. Although between the three of us at Cambridge we ran our vehicle from a station level, as did other areas, any major decisions would rest with him and this wasn't happening. I took the decision to resign from the RRV as I figured this would be the only way to highlight the problem. I put together a letter that basically slated the deployment plan that had been put together by whoever. I made it quite clear that this resource was a waste of money and was being used inefficiently. I gave six weeks notice and sent it off to Glynn. I still enjoyed being on the RRV and felt saddened that I had to take such steps.

With the hours of boredom on my hands I started to educate myself a bit more with something called 'the team leaders development programme. Throughout East Anglia we were to have a huge shake up of the way the different shifts were run. Presently we had five shifts, blue, green, yellow, red and white all manned with six staff. One of those being the Leading Ambulanceman (the boss). All personnel on the shift started and finished at the same time manning three vehicles, and they would hand over to the oncoming shift who would man the same three vehicles. All this was set to change. The Leading Ambulanceman were to be binned and replaced with 'Clinical Team Leaders' (CTL). We would no longer have shifts of six, as these would be replaced with teams of ten inclusive of the CTL. But to become a CTL we had to go through the CTL development programme. This was run over a 6-month period in our own time. It consisted of eight parts to the programme each part being a 2-hour lesson. It covered topics like Health and Safety, Staff Support, Human Resources, Vehicle Working Hours, Deployment Plans etc, I think you get the idea. And it was to finish with an exam. With no management training in the past, apart from running the odd shift, and the three of us running the Cambridge RRV, I had very little management experience. I found it all a bit of an endurance. But with time on my hands while on stand-by out in the sticks, it seemed the ideal opportunity.

I was sitting on stand-by a couple of weeks after resigning from the RRV when the mobile phone rang. "616"

"Hello Chris, It's Glynn"

"Morning" My heart was in my mouth. I knew what this was going to be about and I wasn't too sure how much Glynn had to do with setting up the deployment plan. Having been one of Glynn's victims in the past it wasn't something I wanted to repeat.

"Chris I've received your letter of resignation and I have to say I'm a bit disappointed. Why haven't you spoke about this before?"

"I have Glynn, a few times. But that's where it ends, there's never any further communication"

"Who have you spoken to?" I didn't want to drop my boss in it as I got on really well with him and understood what pressure he was under so avoided the question.

"The thing is Glynn this vehicle must be costing the best part of what, £125,000 a year to run? and we're not doing £125000 of work. The deployment's all wrong and it's not helping out with the on-scene times as its supposed to. Let alone how boring it is sitting in a bloody lay-by eight hours a day, its doing my brains in mate, it needs to change" I could hear Glynn having a little chuckle on the other end of the phone and wasn't quite sure why.

"OK Chris I got that message from your letter. We're having a meeting at HQ about the Cambridgeshire deployment plan in a week. How about you come along and listen in?"

"Yeah, sounds a good idea to me"

"And in the mean time I'll put your resignation on hold if that's OK"

"That's fine Glynn providing it still remains active. Because if I do this for much longer I'll go barking mad" Glynn laughed

"Yes we'll keep it active, don't worry about that. So see you in a week then" we terminated the conversation and I sat back in the car wondering who had come up with the deployment plan? And the meeting thing, was this just a lamb to the slaughter? I know managers get a bit pissed off when some unknown urke comes in gobbing off how crap their plans are! Having never been to such a meeting before it felt a bit intimidating but I reasoned I was only going along to listen in. However over the next week I got my act together and did a bit of research about the RRV workload, times, places and boned up on the geographical shortfalls of the ambulances. All stuff that I thought would make for good ammo, should I need it. The more digging I did the worse the deployment of the RRV became obvious. It was quite amazing how inappropriately the vehicle had been used. There was a huge gap in the north villages of Cambridge where the Ambulances couldn't get to in the specified time and there were also a lot of 999 calls in that area. It was clear to me that if the RRV was deployed in that area it would be an asset to the overall performance of the service and almost a necessity for the patients in that area. They clearly weren't getting the timely treatment that they were entitled to.

The day of the meeting arrived and I was on a 0700-1500 shift. I had explained to control I was due at a meeting but would remain operational should they need me. In the meeting room were 15 people. Some I didn't know, big wigs all suited and booted. They got paid lots of money pontificating about issues greater and wider for me to understand, but wouldn't know one end of a patient from the other. And there were some there that I did know, including Steve my station officer and Glynn who was tapping away at his laptop.

The meeting kicked off with the minutes from the last meeting which was lost on me, I had no idea what they were talking about. Something to do with the strategic planning team! I was expecting the fleet air arm to pitch up outside! We all got issued with deployment plans for the various areas, these are clear rules and locations for deploying vehicles. Then someone opened up the meeting with the phrase "OK lets start with the Cambridgeshire deployment plan" that was quite handy for me as I knew what that meant! This'll be interesting.

Glynn spoke up "I think Chris may have something to say about that" Gulp! I'm only here to listen in I thought, OH well in for a penny.

"Morning everyone. I can't speak for the whole of the Cambridgeshire deployment plan as I don't know enough about the ins and outs of it. But I would like to highlight a problem with the Cambridge RRV deployment plan. Presently we are deployed at 0700 to the North West of Cambridge basing ourselves at the junction of the M11 and A14. This is totally the wrong place to be. If" I got cut short mid-sentence by a guy called Martin. I knew his name but we had never met. He also carried the nickname "The Rodent" owing to the fact he was a pest! He was partly responsible for having ambulance crews standing-by in lay-by's for hours on end, just in case there was an incident.

"The problem with you lot on the Cambridge RRV is that you sit around on station all day" that was not the best thing for me to be hearing amongst the present company.

"Sorry!" I replied slightly raising my voice. There was an instant atmosphere in the room and you could of heard a pin drop

"The Cambridge RRV is renowned for spending more time on station than out on the road"

"I don't think so"

"So what do you think then?"

"I'll tell you what I think we do. At 0700 or there abouts, after checking the vehicle, we deploy to the M11 as I was explaining. And there we sit until we get returned for our half hour break. In the mean time we're available for anything control wish to send us on"

"No you don't, I've seen the evidence. You spend most of your time on Cambridge station" This was not what I expected. I knew the other guys on the RRV at Cambridge, and there's no way they would have sat around on station. And the research I'd done running up to this meeting, would absolutely back us up. He was lying but I didn't understand why.

"Just bear with me for a minute" I picked my back-pack up which had a months worth of RRV vehicle journey logs in it which I had been using for the research. I took them out and looked at the first one. As sure as eggs are eggs it was how I was trying to explain it. I read out the top sheet "0715 stand-by M11, 0830hrs red call, 0915hrs back onto stand-by M11, 1140hrs Cambridge station for a meal break, 1235hrs M11 stand-by. That's the last entry until the end of the shift"

I looked at the next one from a late shift and continued.

"1520hrs stand-by M11" so on and so forth.

"So if what your saying is correct this little lot will be fraudulent then?" I walked to where he was sitting and placed the sheets in front of him.

"Feel free to look through them" he briefly looked through two or three and went on

"I don't know why you go out to the M11 anyway?"

"How about because that is what's written in the deployment plan?"

"No It isn't!"

"Yes it bloody-well is" in my usual diplomatic way. "Look it's written here" I picked up the Cambridge deployment plan and read it out

"0700 following vehicle daily inspection the Cambridge RRV will be deployed to the M11" the room started to rustle as all the others in the room were by now thumbing through the deployment plan.

"But that's not what it means" words escaped me for a moment. I couldn't believe what I was hearing.

"So what exactly does it mean then?"

"It means that you are deployed as early as possible"

"To the M11"

"No"

"But that's what it says"

"But that's not what it means" I bowed my head and shook it from side to side. I looked back up at him "I must be missing the point here somehow" I repeated the question, "So what exactly does it mean then? Come on give me an answer that I understand" I had started to frown and was getting a bit feisty. Glynn spoke up "Hold on Chris. Martin perhaps you can expand on the RRV deployment point?"

"All we're trying to do is get the RRV out as soon as possible. It doesn't necessarily have to go to the M11"

"So why didn't you tell us who are working on the RRV then?" he chose to ignore me but took a verbal swipe at me via Glynn.

"The RRV at Cambridge for what ever reason hasn't been performing as well as we expected" Git!

"I think Chris may have something to say about that as well" Said Glynn.

I went on "Its quite simple" I looked at Martin.

"You've already agreed that the RRV isn't doing what you expected, so lets bloody change it. Consider this. If we deploy to the North of Cambridge at 0700 to a village called Milton the other side of the A14, we can dive onto the A14 to cover all the villages East and West. Its easy access to the North villages and we can also cover the north of the city, which is another shortfall we have for the ambulances. This way we get the times we're required to, the patient gets proper treatment and we don't get bored sitting around in lay-by's"

"So you are having a lot of time doing nothing then" said Glynn

"Yes, look at your desktop and call up the jobs that 616 have done. You'll be lucky to find five per day" Glynn clicked away and looked up. "He's right" Glynn knew I was right but wanted to back me up after Martin had tried to assassinate me.

"This new deployment plan you're talking about is standard system status management" someone else said. What are they going on about I thought to myself, it's a different language. "You can call it what you want. But from an urke on the road I'm telling you this will be more efficient and more cost effective"

"Yes system status management" I felt myself frown again and start to get all defensive.

"Look I'm telling you that this deployment" Glynn butted in "Chris its OK. What Claire is trying to explain is what the service call System Status Management. It's the way the service deploy vehicles to achieve the times laid down by the government. It's a standard system that you've come up with nothing fancy like, moving vehicles around to cover each other, that sort of thing. Its one vehicle with one purpose that's all she's trying to say"

"Arh, OK, sorry about that"

Glynn continued "has anyone else got any other thoughts about the new deployment of the RRV from Cambridge station?" silence "No, OK then" Glynn looked at me "How long would it take to get this up and running then?"

"Now!"

"Now! You'll have to speak with the rest of the team first to see what they think about it and work out a suitable stand-by point"

"We've already discussed it, several times. The stand-by point will be at Milton Country Park it's like a little oasis. There are facilities there we can use and its something we all agree on. Besides, one of them is in hospital after an RTA and the other is off long-term sick, so there's only me. It's not going to be a problem. If it makes life easier why don't we trial it over a six month period. With a review after four months?"

"Yes, that sounds good. Can you get something written down so we can inform control formally?"

"Yes, I'll do it when I get back to the station and E-Mail it to you"

"Good that's finished with then"

"Superb, if its OK I'll be off and get myself back on the road. I wouldn't want to be accused of sitting around!"

I wished everyone good day and made my way to the car. It was a twenty-minute conversation and it was simple. I couldn't help thinking that sometimes the workforce get ignored to the detriment of all involved and because there are people who will not stand up and be counted when a mistake has occurred. We're all only human after all. Control asked me to go and stand-by at the M11. I phoned and explained that the M11 stand-by point was history and I was going to Milton Country Park via station. That afternoon I drafted up a new deployment plan and E-Mailed it to Glynn. It was only a few days before it became a formal stand-by point. The stand-by point was very refreshing. No longer sat in a hotel car park but in a country park. With people and trees and dogs, almost civilised. And we were now getting a decent workload. The downside to this was that I had little time to revise for the CTL development programme. So once again evenings were spent with my head buried in the books.

Chapter 14

Although Milton had become the main stand-by point we still got pulled around into other areas when the cover from the ambulances had been reduced due to the lack of jobs. I was on stand-by to the very west of our area in a little village, it was 12:30am and I was due to finish at 0100am. Control called me *"Control to 616, red call over"*

"616 go ahead" He gave me a job about 15 miles away to the south of our area to a male who had collapsed. *"616 all received over"* Off I went down a main 'A' road that I needed to take for approx five miles. As I came off of a roundabout onto an open clear road I accelerated to about 100mph. Just before I was approaching an army Barracks the dashboard lights came on and the vehicle lost power. In a futile attempt to start the engine again I changed down to fourth gear and let the clutch up to spin the engine, nothing. OK, It's broken! It was dark, cold and misty and I didn't fancy being out in the elements for the next few hours waiting for recovery. At that point I was approaching the entrance to the barracks, that'll do for shelter. I was still doing about 60mph. I dragged the steering around to the right this was now heavy due to the lack of power, likewise the brakes had been affected. I turned into the Barracks at quite a rate of speed and not wanting to block the main entrance I bounced up the kerb and came to a sudden halt just before the barrier. The engine was smoking quite profusely and this, combined with the fog and blue lights flickering, all looked a bit dramatic. I sat for a second gathering my thoughts when there was a knock at the window from one of the guards "you all right mate?"

"Yeah, I think the engines blown up" he looked at my uniform and then the car.

"Oh you're a paramedic!"

"Yes mate"

"Oops, I thought you were the cops, I thought you'd been attacked so I've called for the rapid reaction force"

"Oh my god!" at that moment a Range Rover came hurling around the corner from within the Barracks virtually on two wheels, screeching and wobbling around. It skidded to a halt and six blokes got out dressed in combats, complete with weapons and, ran over to my car while cocking their weapons. Oh my god I'm going to die, I thought. "You all right mate?" "Yes I'm fine, I think the engines blown up" he also looked at the uniform and the car. "You're a paramedic"

"Yes mate I think your colleague thought I was in trouble"

"Yeah I did, I thought he was the cops!"

"Oh well so long as your OK" there was a general sigh of relief and nervous laughter throughout the rapid reaction force once they realised that today wasn't the day they were going to be shot at! I called up control and waited for recovery.

The reason for the RRV blowing up apparently was due to one of the valve adjustments being wrong. With the constant high revving of the car over the past couple of months it had worked loose and the valve had hit number three piston. Number three piston was then found in the exhaust pipe in a million bits! Still it warmed up the rapid reaction force.

With the new stand-by point we'd had plenty of work but nothing too taxing. I'd just arrived at our stand-by point north of the city in the country park. It was a gorgeous sunny afternoon and I was sat on the grass about to get stuck into some revision work that I'd taken with me. The radio sparked up:

"Control to 616 are you receiving over" I jumped up and answered the radio.

"616 go ahead"

"616 can you go red to the A10, we're receiving details of an RTA involving a motorcyclist and a lorry. Your back-up is coming from Cambridge Ambulance Station over"

"616 Roger to that" the location they had given me is a wide piece of road with a speed limit of 60mph. It has quite wide grass verges either side and isn't in a built up area. It can be a quick piece of road and there are a few small roads off of it that lead to villages, these tend to catch motorist's

out. It was about a 30 second drive from my location. I dumped all my paperwork on the back seat, jumped in the driver seat and away. As I arrived at the location I could see a rigid lorry at 90o to the road that looked as if it had pulled out from a junction on my left. Towards the back of the lorry and a bit further down the road was a motorcycle that was quite obviously bent, and just the other side of this was a group of people, some waving at me and others seemed to be crouched over the motorcyclist. As I drove past the huddle of people to park I could see that CPR was in progress. I flipped the boot open with the switch inside the car and came to a standstill. I went to the back of the car and grabbed both bags plus the de-fib. I got down at the head end of the lifeless patient, unzipped my bags and grabbed the ventilation kit. The person who was doing the compressions stopped. I felt for a pulse, this was absent so asked her to continue. There was two or three people giving me information about the collision but I chose to ignore them at this stage so that I could manage a quick assessment of my own.

I pushed an airway into the patient's mouth to keep his tongue forward and his airway partially open. Then as I placed the mask over his face and made an airtight seal with my left hand I could feel that his jaw was broken in several places. I opened his airway by attempting to lift his jaw slightly and could feel very little resistance from his neck. I gave him a couple of inflations and I was happy that his airway was clear. He was cyanosed in colour and was making no respiratory effort. I gave him a couple of inflations and watched for the rise and fall of his chest. This didn't look great but hard to be sure with all the clothing still in place.

"Did anyone see what happened?"

"Yes I saw what happened" said a female to my left.

"Tell me what you saw please"

"The motorcyclist was coming down the main road and the truck pulled out from the left. The Motorcyclist skidded and hit the lorry where the fuel tank is and then went under the truck. I think the rear wheels went over the rider"

"OK thanks. Who was the first person to him please?"

"I was" said the female doing compressions.

"Was there any signs of life when you got you him?"

"No he was still and lifeless"

"Did you start CPR straight away?"

"Yes"

"Is anyone else hurt at all?"

"No just this one"

"Thanks" In between ventilations I opened up the rider's clothing, put the de-fib pads on and switched it on, I asked her to stop the compressions. I wasn't surprised to see a flat line. I gave a couple more ventilations and could see that his chest only had a slight rise and fall to it and was also looking puffy. As I moved my hand over the sides of his chest I could feel air bubbles under the skin. A bit like squeezing bubble wrap they have a popping feeling to them. *This is something called surgical emphysema. If you have a punctured lung air escapes from your lung into the space between your lung and the inner lining of your chest wall. It looks as if you've had an allergic reaction to something and all your body is swelling up. Usually and in the early stages you would only find surgical emphysema on one side and close to the site of the damaged lung. But on this occasion it was all over his chest and ribs and in a very short space of time. Punctured lungs can be as a result of the lung tearing either by itself or by ribs fracturing and puncturing it.*

As I put a bit more pressure on his chest I felt his ribs moving around freely on both sides with a grinding feeling under my fingers. As I looked further down his body his pelvis was at an unnatural angle to his torso. I asked for the compressions to be continued. For the next 30 seconds or so I pondered about the mechanics of injuries that this motorcyclist had gone through. I reasoned that he had probably hit the lorry at 50-60mph. The fuel tank would have been at chest height and has created a lot of the trauma to his ribs, chest and lungs. With the sudden deceleration caused by the impact it's feasible that this had broken his neck. With him now wrapped around the fuel tank gravity has done its thing and he had fallen to the floor where the rear wheels of the lorry had gone over his pelvis, abdomen and probably his lower chest adding to the trauma he has already received.

The person doing the compressions turned out to be a nurse. I looked at her "I think this is going nowhere" she nodded in agreement at that point. We stopped resus and made a mental note of the time. I walked back to the RRV to call control.

"Control this is 616"

"616 go ahead"

"616 you can stand the crew down this is a fatal with no other casualties over"

"616 roger to that" about 30 seconds later I heard sirens and figured that was the crew so made my way up the road to meet them.

"Afternoon guys. This motorcyclist has hit the lorry at quite a speed and has got some serious damage to his chest, pelvis and neck. With the injuries I can see it looks like he died instantly. I've called an end to the resus, as there's too much damage to him for it to be viable"

"OK, you won't be wanting us then"

"No mate, I have just stood you down" with that control called the vehicle and asked them to stand down.

"Ok we'll leave you to it then"

"See you soon" they turned round and left me on scene to get on with the usualtie-up's that we have to do with the police at a fatal RTA.

All the formalities done and I found a shady corner out of the way of the public and stole myself a bit of time to have a smoke and calm down. As I sat on the barrier thinking through what had happened a realization struck me. It's not unknown for ambulance crews to recognise death at the scene of an RTA but if some form of litigation should follow the crew can back each other up and corroborate information. However on this occasion I had no crewmate and I probably foolishly stopped the crew prior to them seeing the patient. This was a huge worry as these days it seems if you look at someone in the wrong way they try to sue you.

The following day shortly after dinner I made a point of going down to the mortuary knowing full well that's where the body would be. I went to the office and knocked at the door "come in" as I opened the door there was four people, three I knew to be mortuary technicians and one who I didn't know. "Afternoon" I said

"Good afternoon. Were not expecting a body are we?"

"No, I've come to follow up a job I did yesterday. A motorcyclist from an RTA"

"Oh yes said a women, I did the post mortem this morning. What do you want to know?" so that was the Boss! I told her the story and highlighted my concerns, which were that I stopped a 'resus' and was it the right thing to do? "Come out here lets take a look" we walked over to a body that was lying on a porcelain slab and had been emptied of its various organs. As we peered into the empty cavity she pointed. "If you look here he has two fractured vertebrae high up in his neck at C3 and C4, these have severed his spinal cord and would have pretty-much stopped any respiratory effort. If we look a bit further down he has also got fractured vertebrae in the middle of his back these have also severed his spinal cord and would have probably caused permanent paralysis if he hadn't already stopped breathing. His pelvis, if you look, is in four bits and there was a lot of blood in the pelvic cavity. This had come from his liver that had been lacerated. He's also got five fractured ribs on the left side. The ribs have fractured in two places allowing them to become detached from anything and move around freely. As a result they have penetrated his left lung. On the other side he had four ribs fractured, also moving around on their own and had punctured his right lung. His jaw was in many bits and he had got a fractured skull. So do you think you did the right thing?"

I took a deep breath "Err probably!"

"Yes absolutely. This chap died very quickly and with irreversible injuries. It was absolutely the right decision. Would you like a cup of tea while you're here?" We headed back to the office and sat down. "I'd like to hear more about the RTA" the boss sat down and ordered two teas and got her sandwiches out! We had a brew and spoke about the RTA over the next 20 minutes or so. When I left the mortuary I was feeling a lot more comfortable about my decision but it was a lesson learnt for the future. Don't try and do everything on your own cause it'll backfire.

Chapter 15

I knuckled down with the revision for the CTL's programme and had got confirmation of an exam date in 10 days time. On the morning of the exam we all had the usual pre-exam questions that everyone experiences, such as what marking system is going to be used and most importantly what is the pass mark? This still hadn't been agreed on! How can that be? You're going into an exam and you don't know what the pass mark's going to be. A bit confusing to say the least. However we cracked on for the two hours, scratching heads, grunting and groaning while covering multi-guess questions. When it was finished we all were released from the exam room and had the usual exchange of notes. Everyone was a bit peeved about not knowing what the pass mark was going to be but what the hell, it's finished with now. We had to wait for the results and from that, 'X' amount of people would be short-listed to go onto the final part which was an inter-view and presentation. After a few days I received a letter through the post to say I had passed and that I'd been short-listed for the final part. I was a bit surprised and there was still no mention of a pass mark. The final part was to be a presentation about various cardiac conditions to a panel of four officers and lasting about an hour. This would be immediately followed by the interview lasting approx half an hour. All prepped and ready to go, I turned up at the HQ to give my presentation and to take on whatever grilling I was about to encounter. I'd never done a presentation before but I reckoned that all the candidates before me would have gone for the usual Power-Point presentation, so instead of boring the panel with another one. I printed off the information onto A4 paper and made a small file for each of the examiners to browse over as I banged on about stuff they had already been subjected to all morning. I was invited in and introduced to all of the panel, two of whom I already knew and two that I hadn't met before, one of them being an instructor from another service. Before I started I explained my reasons for not going for a Power Point presentation and gave them each a copy of the file I'd produced. Apart from being unable to get my words out smoothly in the first minute or so due to the nerves, all seemed to go to plan. After finishing my presentation I was reasonably happy that I'd managed to keep their attention throughout. The panel started with their questions some of which I was expecting and some I wasn't. For the trickier questions I took my time, thought and then responded. The half an hour turned into three quarters of an hour and seemed like it was never going to end. I was relieved when they finally informed me that the interview was complete. I was invited to put any points across that I wanted but I declined, I just wanted to get out and grab a brew. I sat outside for a while having a brew and generally relaxing before heading home.

All of us who had been short-listed and interviewed had been told we would be called into the office and told if we had been successful or not and this would take a few days. I know how the service works when giving out the final promotion results. They inform the successful staff first and then the unsuccessful ones. They attempt to do this all on the same day so those who are not successful can't get wind of the results by a third party. So I figured that no news was bad news, particularly if I got a call in the late afternoon. A few days had passed and I'd had no contact from the service. In my heart of hearts I figured I'd been unsuccessful. Finally I received a phone call at about 4.30 in the afternoon to go to station to speak with Steve our station officer. Given the time of day the only news I was going to hear was going to be bad. I arrived at station with my heart in my mouth prepared for a big ole talk about you did really well but unfortunately you've not being successful on this occasion. I walked up to the office and popped my head around the door, "Evening"

"Hello Chris, come in and close the door" I shut the door and turned to take a seat. Steve was now about two paces in front of me and held out his hand "Congratulations Chris. You are now the meat in the middle of the sandwich" I shook his hand a bit stunned "you mean I've got the job?"

"Yes mate" I felt a big ole grin across my face

"Superb! Who else has got the jobs?"

"Well they haven't been informed yet. But stick around they'll be here soon. Not a word in the crew room though eh?"

"No problem" I went and grabbed a brew and tried to keep a low profile as best I could. I saw three other cars arrive over the next half an hour and surmised they were the guys who had been successful. After a while one of the other guys came into the crew room and called me back up to the office. The four of us that had been successful were now in Steve's office. We congratulated each other and then sat down for a pep talk from Steve about how we were going to organise the teams, vehicle allocation and rota changes etc. This went on for an hour or so and then we all went our separate ways. It was also a way of keeping us on station and away from prying questions from the troops while those who had been unsuccessful could be notified, albeit by phone and not face to face as was the original plan.

We had been given a month to organise ourselves into teams and notify staff what team they were going onto and who their crewmate would be. For the staff this was quite an uncertain time. Those who had long-term crewmates were potentially going to be split and given a new mate. This may sound a bit petty but a bloody good crewmate is what you need. Imagine having to work 12 hours a day, in an ambulance, day in, day out, with someone who you don't actually get on with! You'd hardly look forward to going to work. I was lucky, everyone on my team I knew well and knew they were all good people, except one! And guess who was going to get him as a crewmate? Yup, me! With the remainder of the team I was able to pair them up with other staff they got on with both socially and/or professionally and it only remained for me to get them all on station to break the news.

It took a few days to organise but I managed to get all the team together on station to let them know who was going to be their future crewmates. In the mean time other issues had moved on. The guy I was going to be working with had pulled out of the team as he'd now decided he didn't want to work 12 hour shifts, or maybe he didn't want to work with me! We replaced him with a guy who had transferred from another station, a guy called Al or Big Al!

He stands just over 6 ft and clocks in around 16 stone. We had met briefly a few months before while I was temporarily running a shift and lets just say it wasn't the smoothest of meetings!

So all the team had been called in one by one and given their crewmates, all of which went down as well as I'd hoped. The last person in was Big Al who I think already realised I was to be his new buddy!!! He didn't exactly smile when I gave him the good news, more of a grimace really. All the formalities sorted and we were up and running. The first morning had arrived and Al and I were together. The first few hours were a bit awkward but we soon got to realise we had more in common than our first meeting had had the opportunity to show. We both enjoyed the important things in life like, fast food, beer, the odd bit of totty spotting and station politics (NOT). He'd got a wicked sense of humour and was able to drag me back when I was about to explode at someone. I was able to trust him with confidential information and get a balanced opinion. Soon we had an excellent working relationship and an even better friendship outside of work, drinking copious amounts beer at local beer fest's, discos and clubs. And whilst at work consuming mountains of bacon butties and breakfast rolls! Well we work for the NHS, of course we know what's good for us!

Chapter 16

The county had been gripped by freezing temperatures over the past two weeks with roads, rivers and lakes all freezing over. Al and me had been on a very cold 7am start. It was now 11am and it was time for the usual breakfast roll from the local butty wagon. As we stood talking to the bloke behind the counter the warmth from the stove was a welcome addition and the mouth-watering wafts of the cooking bacon filled the air. Our bellies were rumbling and looking forward to the imminent arrival of our breakfast rolls. Then our handheld radios sparked into life

"Control to 973 are you receiving over" Al and me looked at each other, surely not?

"973 to control go ahead over".

"973, I've got a red for you over" I thought Al was going to burst into tears.

"973 go ahead".

"973, if you could go red to the country park we have reports of someone drowning over"

"973, roger will do.

"I'll leave ya rolls on the hot plate boys, you can pick em up later"

"Cheers Tony" This had all become well-practised, as this wasn't the first time we'd had a shout half-way through one of our various orders.

We jumped into the vehicle and made our way to the country park. En-route we heard an RRV being despatched to the same location. I knew that the RRV had two people on it this morning, as one of them was going through his RRV familiarisation training. This would be helpful should this turn out to be a resus. After eight minutes or so we arrived at our destination and were greeted by a member of the public.

"Morning, where do we need to go?"

"You're fine just here. We've got the guy out of the water but he's really cold and shaky. One of the Park Rangers is bringing him over" shortly after the Ranger approached us with a male roughly in his 60's with grey thinning hair. He was about six feet tall and wearing gold rimmed glasses. He was fully clothed and soaked from head to foot. He was also crying. The Ranger had put a blanket around his shoulders. Not your average suicide I thought.

"Hello Sir, what can I call you then?" I got no reply. With that the fire service arrived on scene.

"OK let's get you into the ambulance and get you warmed up" We'd cranked the heating up on the way to the job so it was all nice and toasty when we got into the back of the ambulance. We sat the guy down and continued.

"Lets get your clothes off mate" We started to strip him to the waist. Whilst not taking anything away from the Ranger as he was doing his best, but there's very little benefit putting dry blankets over wet clothing in freezing temperatures. All it winds up doing is locking the cold air in with very little warming properties and it also makes your blankets wet. After we'd got the patient's clothing off, dried him off and warmed through it was time to get to the bottom of the story.

"So what can I call you then Sir?"

"Jeff"

"OK Jeff, what's happened this morning?"

"I was trying to save my dogs"

"You're dogs! What happened?"

"I have, or at least had, two Westies puppies. They saw some ducks in the middle of the lake on the ice so they went chasing them. As they got to the ducks they realised that the ducks were in a hole in the ice. One of the dogs stopped and began to come back but the other kept going. She disappeared into the water. I ran onto the ice to save her but it gave way. I tried to make my way to her but I couldn't get through the ice. While I was swimming I started to have trouble breathing, so I turned back and had to leave her" with that he started to cry again almost inconsolably. We heard the RRV arrived and Al jumped out to give them a sit-rep (situation report). I was at a loss what to say, being a dog owner myself. And anyone who owns a dog could understand the anguish this guy was feeling.

"What's happened to the one that came back?" He shrugged his shoulders, he didn't know. From a medical point of view there was nothing that we could do for this patient apart from warm him through and TLC. By the same mark we couldn't just turn him out on the street.

"Do you live locally?"

"Yes about a mile away"

"Is there anyone at home?"

"Yes my wife, the Ranger is going to call her" I busied myself with small talk, reassurance and paperwork then I heard some rumblings outside that the dog had been found. "Excuse me a minute" I got out of the vehicle and approached the fire service. "Did I hear something about a dog being found?"

"Yes, the Ranger's got her over there" and pointed towards the Ranger. I walked over to the Ranger who had got this little white bundle wrapped up in another blanket. "Hello again, can I borrow that?" The Ranger passed the little trembling bundle to me.

"Do you know there's another one out there?"

"Yes the fire service are looking for her at the moment" I walked back to the ambulance. As I got in I said to Jeff "Here's someone who'll be pleased to see you I think" and handed him the little bundle. He was overwhelmed and cuddled it like a long lost child and started to cry and say "I'm sorry, I'm sorry are you OK" I wasn't quite sure where to put myself. I sat quietly in the corner busying myself with more unnecessary paperwork. Once again I heard the rumblings that the other Dog had been found. I made my excuses and left the vehicle again. I approached the RRV Paramedic who was going through his familiarisation. "Bob, have they found the other Dog?"

"Yes, it's dead"

"You sure?" he looked at me quizzically "Have you put it on the De-Fib?"

"No!"

"Well go on then!" he looked at me even more quizzically, somewhat confused with a question mark over his head.

"Well go on then, you've got nothing else to do! You've heard about cold water drowning and how people can be resussed up to an hour after a cold water drowning incident. Go on!" a bit miffed but none-the-less he accepted what I was saying he walked off.

The next part I wasn't present at but it went like this:-

The fire service had spread a tarpaulin out and the RRV team put the Westie in the middle of it. The RRV crew shaved its chest and applied the electrodes from the De-Fib. The tracing from the De-Fib had turned out to be Asystole (Flat line, no cardiac movement) at that point they called it a day, as K9 resus isn't something we're too familiar with! At this point the press who had mustered in the car park with us took a picture of Bob and Mark leaning over the Westie with the De-Fib attached! Classic.

Bob came back over to the ambulance and leaned in "Asystole" was his only remark and gave crooked smile. Oh well fair enough, worth a try I thought.

By this time Jeff's wife had arrived on scene and they had been reunited. Jeff, understandably, was still very upset at arriving with two dogs and going home with only one. But nothing could be done that was going to help him in A+E department. He needed a stiff drink and warming through in the comfort of his own home with his wife. We bade them farewell.

We made our way to where the fire service and RRV boys were. There was some light hearted banter/Mickey taking aimed at me to start with but Mark backed me up "Bloody right, if that was my Dog in the same situation and I had the kit, I would of wired him up as well" Some months previously Mark's dog was choking on a piece of meat which the dog couldn't shift. So Mark got a pair of forceps and dragged it out of his throat. A brave move with a choking Alsatian.

To top the job off, the evening papers head lines read:- Paramedics perform CPR on a drowning dog, with a picture of the boys!

Chapter 17

Al and me were on nights (1900-0700). It had been reasonably quiet and we had been mooching around doing run of the mill work. At about 2300 we received a call to an RTA about four miles away. The location was a long, straight, wide piece of road that is one of the main arterial routes out of Cambridge. It was a national speed limit road and when RTA's happened they were usually quite hard hitting.

"*Control to 989, are you receiving over*"

"*989 go ahead*"

"*We have an update for you. Although details are still sketchy it appears that a car has hit a pedestrian, over*"

"*989, roger to that, thanks*"

"*Further information for you, we have also activated an RRV over*"

"*989 Roger to that also*" this was a bit strange as on this piece of road you just don't see pedestrians. It was out in the sticks with no footpaths and only led to a couple of Villages some 4-5 miles away or to the main A11 heading towards London or Newmarket.

As we approached the scene we could see a car facing towards us on our side of the road with its side lights on. It was parked on a narrow strip of ground between the road and the front hedge of a cottage. As we got closer we could make out that the car had been hit and there was damage to the front of it. As we pulled up on scene our flood light revealed that there were a few people running around in the front of a very dark garden and as our eyes adjusted to the gloom we could see a car upside down with the front facing towards the road. Its driver's door was against a tall hedge that ran from front to back in the front garden. The cottage was set back about 30 feet from the kerb.

One of the people on scene approached us "there's someone lying over there by the hedge" and pointed to about ten feet in front of the car. As I got out I enquired how many casualties there were. "Just the one"

"Is that the car driver?"

"No, this guy was on foot"

"Where's the car driver from that car?" and pointed towards the car that was upside down.

"He's in the house but he's fine"

"Al, can you take a look round and see if there's anything else?"

"Will do." I continued, "What about the car driver from the car parked on the side of the road?"

"That's the person laid over there by the hedge" and pointed at the same person again "But he wasn't in his car he was stood by the gate" as I walked over to the point where I was directed to, I could make out a body lying on his back with his legs in the hedge. There was also something like a shrub against his head.

"Hello mate how ya doing?"

"Not too bad, I'm a bit stuck"

"You are indeed" With the dim light of my pen-torch I scanned up and down his body, most of which looked in order. I took a closer look at his legs which seemed to be mis-shapen. On closer inspection it was obvious there was some damage going on but it was tricky to see with my dim light and his legs had become part of the hedge. Al came across after triaging the rest of the scene "no one else mate, what have you got?"

"This chap has got some obvious damage to his legs but can't really make it out at the moment" I shone my pen-torch towards his legs "He appears fully conscious and orientated but I've only just got talking to him. We could do with some light really" with that the RRV pulled up. They carry an excellent spot light for just such an occasion.

"No problem I'll sort it out" Al wandered off to rifle the RRV for its light source.

"So what do I call you?"

"Brin"

"Hi ya Brin, I'm Chris by the way. Anything hurt you particularly?"

"Just my legs man, they're stinging like a crazy cat" What ever that meant!!

"OK Brin, what I'm going to do is start cutting your trousers away to get a better look at your legs"

"No problem man" I started cutting at his cargo trousers with my pen-torch wedged in between my teeth. This I found not to be best practice as the feeble light from the pen-torch kept flickering on and off for most of the time and I wasn't sure what I was cutting. I got on with a bit of questioning instead.

"So Brin, tell me what happened"

"I was stood at the gate saying goodbye to my friend as I'm off travelling around the world. And this car came down the road hit my car and took me out of the game man. The next thing I know I'm all caught up in the hedge"

"So that's your car parked out the front then?"

"Yeah man" this was information I already knew but gave me an insight as to whether Brin had got any memory loss at all. Al returned with the floodlight and set it up. Now we could see what we were dealing with. Brin was about 18 years old, slim build with dark hair which had been highlighted. He appeared laid-back, with a surfy-dude attitude.

As I looked at Brin's legs there was obvious blood loss and deformity. I started to cut away the trousers from his left leg as this looked to be the least injured out of the two. As I cut down and got to just below his knee there was an obvious open fracture of his lower leg. It appeared that the tibia had come through the skin and had gone back in. This is diagnosed by the presence of a yellow, greasy, fatty tissue which has quite a thick consistency to it. And it's usually around the area of a wound. As I cut further down Brin's trousers I was having to fight with the bush to gain some working area. The bush had some big ole thorns on it which kept sticking into my arms, back, bum and legs. I carefully cut away the rest of Brin's trouser leg which was caught up amongst the bush. Sometimes I had to cut the Twigs and branches to gain further access. Once all of the trouser leg was cut away I could see that Brin also had a dislocated ankle.

I now started on Brin's right leg which was a different ball game all together. His lower leg was at a right angle to the rest of his leg and was tangled in amongst all the bushes and branches. About half way down his lower leg the angle turned back on itself and went skywards. As I got to just below his knee I could see that the skin had been peeled back and there was massive trauma. His lower right leg looked like it had exploded on impact and the only thing holding it together was his trousers. As I cut away I found myself wondering which bit to cut next. Where the branches had broken as Brin landed in the bush, they had gone up his trouser leg and worked there way into the open wound. Because of the initial blood loss everything was tinged with blood including the bush. I slowly cut away what appeared to be bush hoping I didn't make a mistake and cut a disguised tendon or ligament. The more I cut away the more unstable Brin's lower leg became.

I decided to stop at this point "Al we're gonna need a splint before we go any further mate"

"OK mate. Do you want a spinal board as well?"

"Yeah, sound mate" (its normal within the service that if someone has had a big impact like Brin and picked up major injuries. We always treat for spinal injuries. Research has shown that because major trauma brings on a lot of pain it can mask any neck pain that may be present. Net result is if we don't treat for a neck injury and there's one present all the movement could cause obvious paralysis)

"The problem is Al that we need to ease him out of the bush. But we can't do that because that bloody shrub's in the way" and pointed to the shrub up at Brin's head.

"I'll soon have that out of the way"

"You got a mini digger in ya back pocket then?" Al looked at the shrub and looked at the area where the car had come through the hedge. With that he got his six-foot-plus frame up and put his arms around the shrub and then lifted it out of the ground and dumped it some distance away. He then continued to the ambulance to get the rest of the kit. I was impressed.

"Right Brin, my colleague has gone to get some splints and bits. What we intend to do is strap you to a board to completely immobilize you. But first, we need to get your legs out of the hedge and into leg splints"

"Ok dude, you know best" does this man feel no pain at all! He was as cool as cucumber. Al returned with all our various splints and between us we supported Brin's right leg and cut away what appeared to be bracken, slowly moving the splint in place. Once Brin's leg was supported we slid him on to the spinal board and strapped him down. It was just a short walk to the ambulance and once we were inside it we had our first chance to get a good look at Brin's injuries and get some decent observation's on him. Al changed the oxygen over to the main flow and got a BP while I started to take a closer look at Brin's injuries. As I opened the splint up it was complete chaos from his right knee down. There were bits of bracken and leaves all caught up within blood vessels, muscle, tendons and ligaments. The actual bones were smashed beyond recognition. I did what I could to clean out the wound but my thoughts were that this was beyond repair but with someone of Brin's age it seemed all that much worse.

Al gave me Brin's BP which, as expected, was low. Also with Brin starting to warm through he had started to feel the pain kick in. We elected to get some fluids up and give Brin some I/V analgesia. Al cannulated and I ran the fluids through ready for connection. Once Al had finished I handed him one end of the giving set to connect up and went to hang the bag of fluids on the hook. As I let go of the fluids I realized, that actually, I had missed the hook! The bag came crashing down an hit Brin straight in the knackers. Al and me looked at each other with one eye squinted and faces looking like pain. "Arh you fucking amateurs" came the yell from the stretcher!! Three things sprang to mind, first, he was right! second never underestimate how painful a kick in the knackers is! And third Brin was really having a bad day!

We apologised profusely and I very carefully hung the bag on the hook where it should have been in the first place. Brin got slugged with some more analgesia out of guilt more than anything else and we toddled off to A+E. We pre-alerted so the trauma team would be waiting for us when we arrived. We gave them the usual handover, history, findings and treatment etc and they set about their assessment. There was an orthopaedic surgeon (bone specialist or chippy for short!) present who went through Brin's right leg like a chef about to cut the fat out of a loin of beef. As he looked and lifted the various parts of flesh from Brin's leg he kept shaking his head as if to say 'no way'. He walked out of Brin's cubicle and consulted with another surgeon who also took a look. Brin being Brin said "what's happening dudes?" and as if by some strange irony this very well elocuted voice replied quietly "It looks as if were going to have to take your lower leg off"

"What was that?"

"It looks as if were going to have to take your lower leg off"

"Arh bloody hell dude are you sure? I'm supposed to be off around the world"

"Sorry there are no options" with that the surgeon left the cubicle and handed Brin back over to the nursing staff to get him prepped for his op.

Whilst I knew that what was being done was the right decision, it left us with a bit of a hollow feeling. Al and me thinned out and went for a smoke outside. A couple of people who were at the cottage came across to A+E. We quizzed them about what had happened prior to us getting there.

It turned out that Brin and a friend had gone round for a "bon voyage" drink. When they were due to leave Brin's friend had started the car, put the lights on but had gone back into the cottage. Brin stood at the front gate saying good-bye to the home owner when a car had driven into his friend's car and then hit Brin. This made it all clear. If you're driving down the road and you see headlights coming towards you, you tend to aim to the left of them. Unfortunately for Brin the car wasn't on the road and the car driver had got confused. He went to the left of the headlights, mounted the grass and collided with Brin launching him into the hedge.

Brin had obviously got a million and one adventures lined up for his travels and these had all been taken away due to factors beyond his control.

What choices will you make today?

Chapter 18

After working together for 12 months, Al and me had formed an excellent working relationship. We had dealt with many trying jobs, had lots of fun and had sunk many pints of real ale together. But it was time, as all my crewmates seem to do, for Al to move onto pastures new and take a position on the RRV working from another station. This left me once again, with the unenviable task of breaking in another crewmate! Enter Ben! Ben was a completely different person to Al. He stands at 5ft 4in, stocky, an ex-rugby player with a shaven head. He was young and as keen as mustard. Seems to go everywhere at 100mph! He'd got excellent knowledge and was very thorough with his patient assessment. Ben was a trainee and now three months into his 12 month probationary period. He'd spent his time so far on a station out in the 'sticks', not what he wanted or needed. On our first morning together we were trundling up the road on a non-emergency job with me driving. Ben looked at me "what don't you like about working with SAT's (Student Ambulance Technician) then?"

"I don't have a problem with SAT's"

"Don't ya?"

"No! The way I see it, is you've got the latest training that you'll be passing onto me. And I've got the experience to pass onto to you"

"Oh good, well that's Ok then!"

"What the bloody hell was that all about?"

"Oh nothing, someone said you didn't like working with SAT's" I laughed out loud.

"Consider yourself the victim of a wind up mate. There is no problem with me and working with SAT's" from that point on, we got on fine. At least I knew that if there was ever a problem he would be brave enough to tell me. So credit where credit is due it wasn't a bad start. As the months unfolded Ben and me got on really well. Once again there were copious amounts of beer drunk in what Ben had called "emergency beer sessions" In essence if we'd had a rough day at work the chances are that everyone else would have as well. So Ben would run round everyone towards the end of the shifts and quote "emergency beer session tonight" in the club on the hospital complex. It worked, we all went over had a few beers and chilled out. Cracking way to finish the day apart from the taxi fare!

Ben and I were on a night shift and we had virtually demolished the inside of the vehicle with a resus we had just finished. We called 'clear' from the location requesting to go back to station to restock with drugs, tubes, needles etc.

"989 I appreciate your situation but is there anyway you can cover another red for us over?"

"989, we could but we only have limited drugs etc over"

"989, well its not exactly another resus, but it's an RTA, one person reported trapped and possibly fatal. You're the only vehicle I have in Cambridgeshire over"

"Yeah rodge fire away"

"Thanks 989, If you can go up the A10 towards Ely, I'll up date you as the information comes in over"

"989 roger to that" We lit up the blues and made our way. just a few minutes had passed when the radio sparked up again.

"989 a further update for you. It's now reported as possibly a double fatal with two trappings. I'm afraid I have no one else to send at this stage over"

"989, no problem, thanks for the update"

The journey was going to take about 25mins and en-route we heard an RRV get activated on the same job. As we pulled up on scene we could see a car that had been ripped in half by impact and in a ditch. About 200 metres up the road was another still steaming wreck. We could see the RRV to our immediate left and two Ambulance personnel. As we got out of the ambulance, a head popped out of the vehicle in the ditch, it was Al who was with a guy who had been on the service for three days. Al had taken him out on the RRV so he could have an understanding of what its role is. Al shouted across the road "Chris this girl's just gone into a cardiac arrest.

There's one more trapped in here, one trapped in the car up the road and there's two dead in the ditch"

"OK mate, I'll send Ben over to you and go up to the other car" Ben made his way to help Al and I walked up the road with my backpack to the other car. As I approached the car I could see big impact on the front end. All the metal work was either pulled off during impact or had been peeled back exposing the engine. The wheels were at 10 to 2 and the roof on the driver's side had been bent inwards towards the driver. There was a firefighter smashing the windscreen with a crowbar. As I looked through the gap that should of housed the passenger window I could see a male lying across the seats, groaning, on his back and unconscious. He had an obvious wound over his right eye with blood trickling down his face.

Smash! "Woe!" I shouted, the firefighter looked at me stunned. "You're covering him with broken glass"

"But I need to get in"

"No ya don't, I'll get in through the door!" the driver's door had been pulled open by Al so he could gain some access to the driver. I pushed my backpack through to the rear seat and scrambled in after it. Once again I only had my pen-torch for light but noticed that the firefighter had got an angle torch. "Excuse me mate can I borrow your torch please?" he handed me his torch and I looked up and down the driver's body. Al had done a cracking job in the circumstances. He'd managed to get the oxygen on and get a cannula in place before scampering down the road to the other car.

I could see an obvious head injury just above his right eye, probably caused by the driver's side "A" post being bent in. He had noisy deep breathing. I took an airway from my bag and attempted to push it into his throat. His teeth had become clenched, which can be a direct result of a head injury or it can be a sign of the lack of oxygen. I placed a nasal airway into both of his nostrils in order to assist with oxygenation, and wound the oxygen up to full flow. I then cupped my hands around the oxygen mask to ensure an air tight seal. After a minute or so I felt his jaw relax slightly and I was able to get an airway into his throat. Now his breathing was virtually quiet but still deep. I put the pulse oximeter on and checked out his blood/oxygen saturation, this was reading 98%. Cool, that's the airway and breathing sorted. His torso was over the handbrake and this would make life very easy for me to check his chest movement. I exposed his chest which revealed no damage. I got my stethoscope and listened to his chest. Good bi-lateral air entry and movement. I checked his pulse which was slow and full, also indicating a head injury. A quick feel over his shoulders and arms revealed nothing. His legs went into the driver's foot compartment. A quick feel down with my hands and there didn't appear to be any leg injuries. I took a quick look at his pupils. One of them appeared to be a bit sluggish when reacting to light. This is also indicative of a head injury, although it hadn't blown completely which was encouraging. So in essence an isolated head injury but needed to be scanned and treated without delay.

"Excuse me mate" I called to the firefighter who was bent down beside the car, no reply

"Excuse me" no reply

"OI!" still no reply. I whacked him on the back of his helmet with the torch while shouting again "OI!" this got his attention.

"What, what"

"Sorry mate but we need to get this patient out soonest, *Rapid Ex Fella*" this seemed to be the buzz phrase being used lately to indicate that a rapid extrication was required or in lay-mans terms "Lets get a shift on!" He walked off in the direction of the rest of his crew. I waited for the cavalry to arrive to start there clonking, banging and cutting but nothing happened. I'd waited far too long and still no fire service had come to my assistance. "What is going on"? I thought. After approx five minutes I was beginning to get a bit pissed off. I was unable to leave the patient and unable to see anyone within shouting distance. Finally a friendly face appeared at the driver's door "Hi ya Chris, anything I can do to help" it was another ambulance crew arrived on scene "Bloody glad to see you guys. This patients got an isolated head injury, GCS (conscious level. Marked out of 15. The lower the figure, the more ill the patient is!) about eight, we need him out ASAP. I spoke with a firefighter but I seem to have been ignored"

"No problem, we'll get them sorted out. Any kit you need?"

"Could have a suction unit handy in case he starts to chuck up"

"Be back with ya in a jiffy"

Within 30 seconds the sector commander from the fire service was with me.

"Hi ya mate what do you need?"

"I need this patient out ASAP, he's got an isolated head injury and he's not trapped"

"Which way out do you want to come?"

"Probably best if we take the nearside 'off'. We can slide him straight onto a board then"

"Yup that's do-able" off he trotted and I could hear the orders being barked out as only the Fire Service do. Within a minute the well oiled machine of the Fire Service spun into action. They jemmied open the front and rear passenger doors, snipped the hinges and removed the doors completely. They then snipped the top and bottom of the "B" post and removed that out of the way. Within 3-4 minutes we were well on the way to being out of the car. The ambulance crew that had arrived on scene had organised the stretcher and spinal board and between us and the Fire Service we removed the casualty from the car methodically and smoothly. Once we got into the ambulance we reassessed the patient. His clenching hadn't returned and his blood/oxygen saturation was still in the upper 90's. His pulse was still a bit slow but wasn't too bad. Another look at his pupils revealed no change, indicating his head injury wasn't worsening. For the first time I was now able to get a blood pressure. This was slightly high (normal for a head injury) but in the circumstances he could have been in a lot worse shape.

En-route to A+E I gave them a pre-alert so they were ready for our arrival. As usual there was a full trauma team ready and waiting for us. I gave them the handover and went to clean up the vehicle, which by now looked like down-town Beirut! As the story unfolded it turned out that the car was driven by a teenager who had lost control or was on the wrong side of the road. The car turned out to be a 'cut 'n' shut' (two cars welded into one) and fell apart on impact. The three passengers in the back had been ejected at great speed and had all collided with the bank on the far side of the ditch killing them instantly. The girl driving who had gone into cardiac arrest on our arrival, never responded to any resus that was carried out. The other passenger who was trapped in the 'cut 'n' shut' had injuries which were repairable and was later discharged from hospital. As for my patient, after an emergency brain operation he went through a lengthy rehabilitation process and was discharged from hospital some months later. The prognosis was optimistic and hopeful that he would return to full time work. By some strange twist of fate they turned out to be related to each other! Not the way to bump into your relations really!

Chapter 19

When I joined the Ambulance Service back in 1986 it had just about moved out of the dark ages and had relaxed the employment criteria. Up until a couple of years previous they would still only employ married men who had a clean driving licence and some first aid experience. Now the criteria is much tighter. The service are expecting new recruits to have 'O' levels and some form of biology or anatomy and physiology background. This is all very well but actually what is needed along with that is someone who has also had a life other than sitting in a classroom since the age of six being hand fed education. Not necessarily street-wise but worldly-wise, and able to understand people from all walks of life and able to communicate with them. This isn't learned in a classroom.

We've now got as many female staff as male staff and we are all equal within the working environment and the skills we provide to the public. If anything, it improves the resources we can provide. Some patients would favour having a female attend to them, whilst some would prefer a male. This is beneficial, particularly when we're dealing with a complete cross-section of cultural communities. For instance, women from some cultures, will not allow anyone to touch them other than their husbands. We're employing people from all over the world which is perfect for getting over the language barriers that we encounter when dealing with foreign tourists. Currently on station we have a Venezuelan, an Aussie, a Russian, blimey! we're even employing the Welsh!! Just kidding. Obviously they all speak good English but they are happy to undertake some interpretation over the phone when needed. It's also a great education to sit down and talk about their various countries and cultures.

We've become a more technical service now. From the days of basic first aid knowledge with no more than splints and oxygen at our fingertips, to carrying drugs which will reverse a developing heart attack but which equally could kill a patient whilst being administered. There is a huge judgement call that has to be made in the heat of the moment, whilst interpreting that wiggly line known as an ECG. We've moved on from seeing a wound and just dressing it, to seeing a wound, dressing it and replacing the blood that has been lost. Some of our staff have been away on courses and are able to stitch wounds and dish out antibiotics, which saves a GP the journey. Whilst that type of work interests me, I would have to give up my Team Leader role and mainly be based in a GP's surgery. That's not for me as I enjoy the front line work too much. We now have direct phone lines into the various A&E departments that we use. This is not just for pre-alerting the department to an arriving patient but is also used as an advice line so we can speak either with nurses or doctors to ensure the correct course of action is taken for the patient. For instance, some of the more unusual diseases or syndromes which we might come across might not have to go to the A&E dept, but can be managed quite adequately at home by family. The A&E staff have a far better understanding of these types of illness than us. It's far better for the patient not to be sitting in the A&E dept for hours on end and likewise the A&E dept are not having to unnecessarily use up a bed, happy days!

We have a far better understanding these days of what happens to people during accidents, particularly during RTA's. The forces they endure on impact and how that effects internal organs as well as the external injuries we can see. We work extremely closely with the doctors at RTA's and there's a healthy respect for each other. The down side (there's always a down side eh!) is that because of the research and appreciation of injuries that can occur with crash victims, we send ambulance crews, RRV's, doctors, Ambulance Officers and the odd helicopter to a lot of incidents. Well excuse me for being a cynic but actually we could better organise ourselves and the job would probably go smoother without so many people on scene.

From an aggression side of things, it used to be a question of good 'ole' fashioned fisty-cuffs and maybe the odd 'bottling'. We would pitch up and be a totally neutral participant in the on-going disagreement, patch-up the injured and be on our way. Now there are a lot more stabbings and shootings to be dealt with, and according to the government we should be on scene within eight minutes from time of call. This is quite crucial to patients with a developing cardiac problem and obviously for cardiac arrests. But the flip side to this is that sometimes it's extremely difficult for the call takers to gather all the information that's required and we arrive on scene before we know what's going on. Once whilst on the RRV I was attending a domestic dispute between two neighbours. The patient having been belted around the head with a motorcycle security chain, and whilst dealing with him Control phoned to inform me not to approach the location as there had been trouble there before. They also gave me the road junction which would form the RV point with the police. I explained that I was in the house already. Within a minute or so there was a huge police presence. No harm done on this occasion but 12 months ago one of my colleagues had two teeth knocked out and he is absolutely not Mr aggressive. Unfortunately for the assailant my colleagues dad happens to be a solicitor! OH DEAR!

We're no longer seen as a neutral body but fair game to those who see us as an easy target. Violence towards crews is on the increase with sometimes a detrimental effect on the patients who genuinely need us. For example, if we've been called to the usual pub fight the chances are that we're going to be verbally abused by all who think they understand what we do and know better than us. Arguments are common place between third parties and ambulance crews and seldom is there time to take a breather between jobs. The next call which could potentially be poor 'ole' Doris who has taken a fall and fractured a hip. It can sometimes be difficult to be the professional caring person which we all are, or we wouldn't have started the job in the first place. So should you ever be in the unfortunate position of having to call 999 and the crew turn up with a bit of 'attitude', cut them a bit of slack. They've probably just been used as a verbal punch bag, it won't last long and it's not personal.

We've certainly gone through a lot of different types of vehicles. From the Bedford's which had a set of two-tones on top that filled up with snow and rain and sounded like a strangled cat by the time we got to our location. To the much loved and very reliable handling of the V6 Transits. And as for the 'wobbly buses' from the States, Ooo I can feel my palms sweating up just thinking about them! Currently we're running Mercedes Sprinter chassis cabs, powered by 2.6 TDI engines. Some of the vehicles have got over 200,000 miles on the clock which is testament to the quality of the engines and makes good business sense. But a change of bushes and suspension units at a 100,000 miles wouldn't go a miss, and would give our patients a more comfortable ride. The rear of these are based on the 'wobbly buses' and have a good working area with stacks of cupboard space and light to work with. The radios used to be a whiskey 15. A big 'ole' blue set that perched on the top of the dashboard with two knobs. The up-to-date units are much more sophisticated. Soon to be digital, not that I totally understand the ins and outs of that too well! Each vehicle carries two units per vehicle. One for domestic everyday use and the second for major incidents, this gives us a separate network to communicate by. There is a huge amount of extra radio work that goes hand-in-hand with a major incident, and this leaves the domestic network to continue in its normal way. They are also fitted with a panic button which when pressed turns the controllers screen red and makes it flash. In turn the controller will attempt to contact the vehicle. If there's no reply the police are automatically activated to that location which is identified by a large map screen which sits on the Control-room wall. All the vehicles have 'sat nav' fitted but are not an absolute system to take you to the location in the quickest time. Sometimes a good 'ole' map is the best way.

We also have another system known as 'Terra-fix'. This basically is a system which allows Control to text the jobs through to us and update us without having to take up valuable air time. It's a small screen with a multitude of buttons below it. These are used to send our status to control, i.e. mobile to a job, arrive at scene, leaving scene etc etc. We can also let Control know if we're re-fuelling, re-kitting, on our way to a stand-by point etc. Quite a lot really!

The cockpits of the vehicles are starting to look like a mini version of an aircraft cockpit. All fitted with 'stuff' to make our journey more efficient and ultimately eliminate delays with patient care. The RRV's have brought a new dimension to the service and are great fun to work on. They can take on the role of communicator, assist crews with tricky patients, whether that's with lifting, treatment or bringing extra kit. They can square away social issues with patients by organising doctors or community nurses and Social Service back up when required. This allows crews to be freed up and get back to what they should be doing, taking patients to hospital. But their biggest asset is that they can cover the ground quickly and as you appreciate, time is crucial.

So, to the future!

As I've said over the past 20 years the violence towards crews has increased, so where are we going to be in another 20 years? Will we have to don stab or bullet proof vests? Yup, I reckon we will, and I'll make a chilling and horrible prediction. Over the next 20 years somewhere in this country an ambulance crew or at least part of an ambulance crew will be killed by an unprovoked and cold blooded attack! I've still got over 20 years to go until I retire, so I put myself in that category.

Currently the retirement age is 65. The government is pushing for that to be raised to 70. Would you want to be doing this at 70 years old? Not me! It's a job for younger staff than that. Physically, you need to have reasonable fitness to get into the service in the first place and a lot of applicants fail at that point. But once you're in there are no facilities to maintain your fitness level, so naturally you'll become less fit as you get older. You also need to have a sharp thought process. In the heat of the moment there are calculations that have to be done to work out the correct drug dosages and these all relate to the weight of the patient. A patient's weight can be given in two ways, stones and pounds (lbs) or kilogram's and grams (kg's). All drug dosages are worked out in kilograms. We often find ourselves in the position of trying to convert lbs into kg's and then work out what the correct dosage is, this has to be done in quick time. It's a well-known fact that our thought process slows down as we get older. I would hate to get it wrong but not as much as my patient would!

What about the vehicles of the future? Will they become mini mobile operating rooms? Well why not? I don't mean for every 999 call but there is clearly a category of patients who would benefit from such a vehicle. Currently in major trauma cases we have a number of doctors and supervised paramedics, who can perform open thoracostomies. This is where we slice between the ribs on either side of the chest and push a hole through to the lungs. This allows any internal bleeding that's trapped in the thoracic cavity to be drained off, thus allowing the lungs to fully inflate. This is a relatively common injury with RTAs when a patient's chest has hit the steering wheel. The operation sounds complicated but once performed a couple of times, it is a relatively easy skill and saves lives. So why shouldn't all Paramedics perform it?

Who knows we may even have hover vehicles by then? all running on brussel sprouts! Maybe in the future eh!

As for the staff of the future? Blimey, what a nightmare! All staff at present should be known as paramedics. The EMT's (ambulance staff who haven't sat the paramedic course but are still front line.) have gone through a comprehensive course to get as far as they have, and people tend to forget that they can still administer drugs unsupervised. They can still reverse certain types of cardiac arrest, and they're having to interpret ECGs to the standard of a paramedic so they can either pre-alert their various A+E departments of their arrival and what with, or call for paramedic back-up. Surely if they can do the complicated work they should have the recognition to go with it. But of course as soon as you call an EMT a Paramedic that cost's a couple of thousand pounds a year in wages! So in the future I can see everyone being called a paramedic. The only difference is that we'll probably have grades. For instance, you are grade one paramedic you will be at the same standard as an EMT at the moment with 'maybe' a few more skills, going all the way up to the top, whatever grade that'll be. But this could well be the guys and gals who have gone through their university medical degrees and have decided that working in a hospital or a doctor's surgery isn't quite what they want to do after all. As for the service they'll probably be expecting the new staff to have already done a degree or two, if for no other reason but to be sure the applicants have the intelligence to take on board the extra training and knowledge that will be required by them. But however the future rolls out, the basis of the job will remain the same. Dealing with people who have found themselves in a compromised and unforeseen circumstance and having to work under quite stressful conditions for most of the time. From the homeless with a chest infection to Doris with the fractured hip. From the highs of a successful resus to the meeting of patients like Jessie.

I'll raise a glass to the future but let's not meet professionally!

Lightning Source UK Ltd.
Milton Keynes UK
172774UK00001B/50/A